Drinking Vancouver

Drinking VANCOUVER

100+ Great Bars in the City and Beyond

John Lee

TouchWood
Editions

TouchWood Editions
www.touchwoodeditions.com

Library and Archives Canada Cataloguing in Publication
Lee, John, 1969–
    Drinking Vancouver : 100+ great bars in the city and beyond / John Lee.

ISBN 978-1-894898-96-6

1. Bars (Drinking establishments)—British Columbia—Vancouver Metropolitan Area—Guidebooks. I. Title.

Editor: Holland Gidney
Design: Pete Kohut
Cover Illustration: Richard Simpkins, istockphoto.com
Author photo: Dominic Schaefer

We gratefully acknowledge the financial support for our publishing activities from the Government of Canada through the Canada Book Fund, Canada Council for the Arts, and the province of British Columbia through the British Columbia Arts Council and the Book Publishing Tax Credit.

Mixed Sources
Cert no. SW-COC-001271
© 1996 FSC

This book was produced on 100% post-consumer recycled paper, processed chlorine free and printed with vegetable-based dyes.

The information in this book is true and complete to the best of the author's knowledge. All recommendations are made without guarantee on the part of the author. The author disclaims any liability in connection with the use of this information.

1 2 3 4 5 13 12 11 10

PRINTED IN CANADA

*For my brother Michael,
who certainly likes a beer or three.*

Contents

Introduction

As an expat Brit born with warm pale ale coursing through my cast iron veins, it fell to me to undertake the arduous task of bar-crawling through more than 100 local watering holes. Sometimes I was even sober—although my notes were occasionally on the wrong side of legible the next day. But I didn't just turn a keen amateur interest into a paying gig (yes, I know you hate me) on a mere whim. In fact, there has never been a better time for a book like this one.

A quiet revolution in Vancouver's bar scene in recent years has replaced lame boozers serving fish and chips and Bud specials with a full round of character pubs, wine bars, cocktail lounges and sunset-hugging patio drinkeries. It's a transformation that has paralleled the rise of BC's wine sector and the no-less-exciting renaissance in our regional microbreweries. You can still sip tipples from around the world here, of course, but now's also the time to consider a lip-smacking 100-mile liquid diet.

Whatever you decide to sup on, you'll be honouring a historic line that goes right back to Vancouver's founding. Gassy Jack Deighton, the chancer who arrived with a whisky barrel and built a bar that triggered the development of the modern-day city, stands in jaunty bronze form in the heart of Gastown's Maple Tree Square. While Gastown's fortunes have ebbed and flowed like a tipsy drinker over the years, it's now Vancouver's best bar neighbourhood, lined with appealing taverns that draw the kind of crowds that would make old Jack proud.

But drinking in Vancouver is not just about Gastown. This book is handily divided into 11 neighbourhoods—from Yaletown to Kitsilano and from Main Street to

Commercial Drive—each with a useful map so you can plot your own leisurely crawl: all you need is a group of friends and this slim tome in your pocket. Along the way, you'll find special sections with top drinking, dining and ambience suggestions, as well as recommended pit stops for the next time you're on the road in other parts of BC.

Aside from these side orders, there are 100 main reviews here, a subjective list of what I consider Vancouver's best places to drink. Nightclubs and ticketed live music joints are generally not invited to the party, but those exceptional restaurants that take as much care over their drinks lists as their nosh menus are included where appropriate. And here's my nod to Vancouver's oddball liquor laws: keep in mind that some establishments require the purchase of food under the terms of their licenses.

Each main review paints a picture of what to expect and includes an "essential tipple" and a "must-have nosh" tip. Denoted by a cheery star symbol, 12 bars are also deemed worthy of extra attention: in my opinion they are the sudsy *crème de la crème* of Vancouver drinking spots and should not be missed on any account.

Naturally, you'll have your own ideas about the city's best watering holes (if you ever need a conversation starter, consider debating a personal top five list). And, of course, as with any book like this, there's the built-in problem of obsolescence—bars (and their menus and specials) come and go and some of the ones listed here may not be around when you turn up at the door desperate to wet your whistle. Luckily, I have a solution: visit www.drinkingvancouver.com (or use the slightly more egotistical www.VancouverBarGuy.com) for the latest information on bar openings and closings across the city. You're also invited to send in your own fave recommendations plus share that new beer, cocktail or tapas plate you've just discovered. With any luck, the discussion will inform a future edition of this book. I'll also be posting tipple-related stories on the city and beyond, so it's a real chance to create a community of barflies with something worth slurring about.

For now, though, it's time to hit the road (with a designated driver, of course). Flick through these pages, choose a couple of unfamiliar and appealing spots and get out for a beverage or two. Once you're there, don't forget to drink slowly and deeply. And if you see a slightly dishevelled guy in the corner taking messy notes over a dark beer, it's probably me.

Cheers!
John Lee

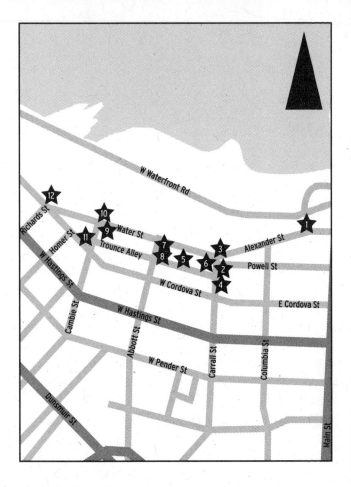

Gastown

Gastown

Since modern-day Vancouver was triggered by the boozy 19th-century settlement that grew up around Gassy Jack Deighton's landmark saloon, it's fitting that the brick-paved Gastown neighbourhood kick-starts this book. But this isn't mere sentiment. While heading for drinks in the city's oldest enclave—designated a National Historic Site in 2009—would have been almost unheard of a few years back (unless you liked a side order of fistfights with your skanky beer), this formerly dodgy skid row has recently been reborn as Vancouver's best watering hole hangout.

Radiating from Deighton's jaunty bronze statue—perched atop a whisky barrel at the junction of Water, Carrall, Powell and Alexander streets—you'll find excellent bars like Six Acres, Irish Heather, Chill Winston and the Diamond, each making good use of their heritage haunt settings. But a Gastown pub crawl doesn't have to begin and end in Maple Tree Square. Tempting yet diverse tipple spots like Pourhouse, Steamworks, Black Frog and Alibi Room will lure you slightly further afield, proving that while the bar-packed Granville Strip may offer more quantity, Gastown is all about quality. It's a revelation that would make old Jack as happy as a thirsty mill worker on payday.

Alibi Room ✪
Vancouver's best bar for BC microbrew fans

Essential tipple Old Yale Pale Ale

Must-have nosh Bison Cheesesteak Sandwich

Coordinates 157 Alexaznder Street, 604-623-3383, www.alibi.ca

A warm and welcoming pilgrimage destination for true BC beer nuts, this laid-back contemporary tavern used to be a humdrum haunt for Hollywood North movie crews (hence the shelf of dog-eared scripts) but it's been completely reinvented in recent years by a Brit co-owner who knows a thing or two about great quaffs. Now, you'll find an ever-evolving roster of regional microbrews—one of the biggest in the city—in a convivial brick-built room that's striped with long communal tables. There's also a cozy subterranean snug downstairs where DJs find their groove on Friday and Saturday nights.

The astonishing array of BC drafts—there are up to 25 taps and three additional revolving casks—changes based on availability as well as the arrival of seasonal brews. But you can expect your beer education to be enhanced immeasurably by lip-smacking treats like Red Racer ESB from Surrey, Swans Extra IPA from Victoria and Crannóg Organic Cherry Ale from Sorrento. And that's before you even consider Phillips Chocolate Porter, Lighthouse Dry Irish Stout and the darkly satisfying Old Yale Pale Ale. Even local brewpubs like Dix, Steamworks and Yaletown Brewing send their most interesting casks here, knowing they'll be savoured by a crowd of young Gastown hipsters and older, beer-ravaged Campaign for Real Ale (CAMRA) drinkers.

Taste-trippers should consider a $9 "frat bat" of four 4oz samples (choose your own or ask to be surprised). And if you're done with BC, there's a 20-strong bottle choice that includes the excellent Barron Dark Lager from the Czech Republic. Eventually, you'll have to concede that beer doesn't quite cover all your dietary needs; luckily there's some good-quality comfort food here to line your stomach for the next session. Skinny fries with chili-garlic vinegar is a great side, while more substantial fare includes free-run chicken curry and a bulging, Pemberton-sourced beef burger. Even better, is the bison cheesesteak sandwich, served with fries and pumpkin-seed coleslaw—it's a good reminder that there's apparently more to life than great beer (no, I don't believe it either).

Diamond

Stylish upstairs gem with a serious cocktail commitment

If statuesque Gassy Jack could step from his whisky barrel perch for an evening of local imbibing, he'd hardly know which direction to turn for a libation or three. If he's smart, though, he'll nip across Maple Tree Square and up the unassuming staircase a few doors in along Powell Street. He'll find a compact, high-ceilinged heritage space lined with exposed red brick and studded with tall sash windows that offer a pigeon's-eye view of the brick-paved spot where his saloon once stood. The sexy Diamond is one of Gastown's newest watering holes, but it raises a respectful glass to the past better than most.

Reinventing a century-old space formerly occupied by the infamous Savoy nightclub (but there's also been a brothel and a speakeasy here), it's hard to imagine a cocktail lounge with a less snooty approach. Arrive early for an evening window seat or tuck yourself into a back wall perch and watch the late-twenties hipsters roll in for a night of convivial chatter. It's an intimate space that warms to a cozy glow as the light wanes outside and the eye-catching chandelier, with its stag-head adornments, takes centre stage.

The Diamond's expert, multi-page cocktail list is divided into Boozy, Refreshing, Delicate, Proper, Notorious and Not So Boozy. Regulars can take weeks to find their well-crafted favourites, which can range from the summer-friendly Buck Buck Mule (gin, sherry, cucumber juice, cilantro and ginger beer) to the winter-warming and highly recommended Penicillin (blended scotch, peated scotch, ginger, lemon and honey). It may not be strictly medicinal, but it cures most ills.

Additionally, there's a petite but carefully chosen bottled beer array that includes treats from Tuborg, R&B and Pacific Western Brewing out of Prince George. Designed for sociable sharing, there's also a small but well-formed Asian-fusion tapas menu (think izakaya) with dish prices invitingly reined in under $10. Selections change based on seasonal availability, but regular favourites include pork gyoza, green-tea noodles, a duck and chicken sub and the excellent pickled beets and egg dish, prepared with Japanese mayo.

Essential tipple Penicillin
Must-have nosh Pickled Beets and Egg
Coordinates 6 Powell Street, www.di6mond.com

Chill Winston

Yaletown-style drinkery with Gastown's top patio

Essential tipple Blanche de Chamblay
Must-have nosh Raspberry Cappuccino Crème Brûlée
Coordinates 3 Alexander Street, t 604-288-9575, www.chillwinston.ca

Dominating Maple Tree Square's northern edge in a landmark 1898 commercial pile, the sprawling patio here is Gastown's best summer evening perch. Drink in the cobbled panorama from behind the railings (squint and it looks like old-school Europe) or, if you're lacking factor-50 sunscreen, duck under a protective parasol. The rest of the year, hit the shaded, brick-lined interior and its multitude of little tables and loungey, leather-look sofas. Chill Winston may be in Gastown but it takes a cool, Yaletown approach to its heritage digs.

The attitude is reflected in its slightly naughty washrooms: a clutch of enclosed individual facilities opening onto a central fountain-style sink where you'll be washing hands and locking eyes with those of the opposite sex. It's slightly odd but it also ensures that those feral males (you know who you are) who usually avoid handwashing are effectively embarrassed into doing so.

You can avoid the washrooms altogether, but only if you're willing to ignore the tempting boutique beer selection, aimed at connoisseurs who wouldn't be seen dead with a Kokanee. Phillips IPA from Vancouver Island, summer-friendly Blanche de Chamblay white ale from Quebec and the UK's lip-smacking "Newkie Brown" (that's Newcastle Brown Ale to non-Brits) are draft highlights, alongside a bottled array including Leffe, Fin du Monde and Anchor Steam Ale. Also ask about the "rare list" of limited-availability brews.

Wine fans are also well-served, with a New World selection from Argentina to South Africa (plus some choice BC tipples). Yaletown expats can also lap up flirty cocktails like Whispering Waldorf, Spooning Jesus and the signature vanilla and peach–themed Sin Winston. Food-wise, the gourmet-flecked menu is similarly diverse, ranging from tuna tartare to turkey wings and a good range of decadent desserts. Full entrees are available, but shareable tapas are the way to go—start with a cheese plate and end by fighting over the excellent raspberry cappuccino crème brûlée.

Irish Heather

Forget leprechaun-lined theme bars,
this gastropub is the real deal

Locals were lamenting the closure of the old Heather even before it shut its creaky doors for the last time in 2008. But despite the new digs opening just across the street the very next day, it soon became clear that this was a reinvention rather than a replica of the beloved former spot. Divided into three distinct areas in an H-shaped layout, Heather 2.0 is Vancouver's best gastropub and its new look symbolizes how best to renovate Gastown.

A high-ceilinged room of exposed brick and hardwood floors made from old Guinness barrels, the narrow main bar is lined with little tables and has a traditional pub feel. Past the passageway washrooms, you'll find a mammoth long table in a second room that's a café by day, before becoming a chatty bar overspill at night. At the back of this room is the entrance to the Shebeen Whisky House. While wistful Heatherites remember the windowless old Shebeen fondly, this new room is more like the carpeted snugs found in traditional UK pubs—luckily, it still serves up Vancouver's biggest whisky menu.

Feel free to start down the slippery slope of around 180 whiskies. Or pace yourself with a beer or two instead. Naturally, this is the best place in town for a properly poured Guinness (yes, you can taste the difference) but you can also wet your whistle with excellent drafts like Smithwick's Red Ale, Howe Sound Nut Brown and R&B Pale Ale. There are some fine bottled beers and ciders too, often including Brooklyn IPA, Fullers ESB, Bulmers Original Cider and the smashing Rogue Brutal Bitter.

As for that second nutrient provider: other bars may offer potpies and bangers and mash but the Heather's are made with gourmet devotion. The hearty steak and Guinness pie is packed with chunky goodness, while the bulging sausages will lag you for a prolonged hibernation. And look out for the Long Table Series: at time of writing, this $12 to $15 dinner-and-beer special was operating Sunday to Thursday and proving to be a runaway success.

Essential tipple Guinness
Must-have nosh Steak and Guinness Pie
Coordinates 210 Carrall Street, 604-688-9779, www.irishheather.com

Salt Tasting Room

Cave of chatty bacchanalians indulging
their wine, cheese and meat fantasies

Essential tipple Poplar Grove Syrah

Must-have nosh Cheese Monger Plate (with piccalilli)

Coordinates 45 Blood Alley, 604-633-1912, www.salttastingroom.com

In a city with a few humdrum eateries masquerading as wine bars, this backstreet gem hits the spot perfectly—and with a commendable lack of pretentiousness. Skip briskly along shady Blood Alley and duck inside the mood-lit, brick-lined cocoon; it's instantly warming and animated with chat—especially if you hit the communal table where you'll be rubbing elbows with fellow bacchanalians.

According to Salt, there are only three food groups—meat, cheese and booze—and they're fully explored in a simple but meaningful approach to indulgence. There's a boutique selection of bottled beers, including Bombardier Ale from the UK and Anchor Liberty Ale from San Francisco, plus a short but sparkling array of spirits (as part of the Irish Heather empire, you can expect good whisky here). But it's the kaleidoscopic retinue of 100 wines, the majority gratifyingly available by the glass, that lures most.

A good diversity of Old and New World selections is offered—including less-familiar BC treats from Blue Mountain, Elephant Island and Venturi-Schulze—plus a plethora of pleasant surprises. Consider a Poplar Grove Syrah from the Okanagan or a light Shepherd's Ridge Pinot Noir from New Zealand, then finish with a substantial slug of sherry from the 20-strong Spanish list.

Food-wise, it's all about cold protein plates. Peruse the blackboard for the day's available cheeses and charcuterie, then choose three (or more) to accompany your libation. The exquisite cured meats, many from Granville Island's celebrated Oyama, often include fennel salami or smoked beef loin; while cheeses can range from delicate Caerphilly to hearty ash camembert from Vancouver Island. All are served with crackers and condiments: do not miss the sharp, neon-yellow piccalilli.

If you're a true hedonist, consider one of Salt's regular winery tasting nights. And look out for the Judas Goat Taberna scheduled to open next door but not quite ready during research for this book. It's the latest tempter in the Irish Heather stable.

Six Acres

Quirky and convivial latter-day tavern
with lip-smacking beer and tapas

Tucked behind Gassy Jack's statue—drink enough and he'll moon you—this lovely brick-lined bar is effortlessly cool without being slavishly hip. Nestled in the Alhambra Hotel building (site of Gassy's second saloon), the coaster-sized patio is summertime-popular, but it's the toasty interior that tempts—especially on rainy nights when Maple Tree Square's heritage streetlamps cast a silvery, old-school glow.

Saloon-chic features here include hardwood floors, comfortably dinged wooden tables and leaning redbrick walls framing oddball accessories like a yellowing globe and vintage ice skates. There's a small library of junkshop books (now's your chance to read *A Terrible Temptation*) plus some battered board games. Unpack Mastermind in the snug-like upstairs area, perched like a minstrel gallery above the small bar.

Stretch your legs with an ablutions visit up here. You'll find fake celebrity photos leading to washrooms that broadcast eccentric spoken-word tapes. On my calls of nature, Hindi language lessons and that Orson Wells' *War of the Worlds* radio production provoked some long, drawn-out handwashing.

The bar's bottled beer roster, on menus encased in old book covers, includes dozens of saliva-triggering possibilities. Take your time weighing options from Spain's Alhambra Lager to Nova Scotia's Propeller Bitter and the UK's rich and satisfying Hobgoblin Dark Ale. There's also a full page of Belgian tipples, plus daily-changing specials (ask about additional unadvertised beer specials). A few choice wines and spirits round out the drinks list, while there's also a noteworthy double-page whisky spread if you fancy a rain-avoiding nightcap.

Soak up all this leisurely imbibing with a selection from the bar's rustic tasting plates, built for sharing. The best two are the Sophia Loren (cured meats, olives, sun-dried tomatoes, herbed chèvre and rosemary bread) and the Olympian (hummus, tzatziki, tabbouleh, lemon potatoes, feta-stuffed tomatoes and warm pita). Order both for an ideal evening feast.

Essential tipple Hobgoblin Dark Ale
Must-have nosh Sophia Loren
Coordinates 203 Carrall Street, 604-488-0110, www.sixacres.ca

Lamplighter
Gentrified heritage saloon for the party-loving crowd

Essential tipple Rogue Dead Guy Ale

Must-have nosh Cajun Chicken and Cheese Sandwich

Coordinates 92 Water Street, 604-687-4424, www.donnellypubs.ca

Vancouverites fondly recalling the old Lamplighter can be guaranteed to wistfully regale everyone with tales of fun fistfights at some cracking live music gigs. But viewing the past through beer-tinted spectacles is an easy way to forget that this cavernous Water Street pub had been flirting with dive-bar status for several years and many locals were guardedly avoiding it. Despite a colourful, decades-long history that includes being the first area tavern to allow women drinkers without escorts, the tired watering hole needed a fresh start.

That's when the Donnelly Pub Group, lovers of all-black interiors, waved their magic gentrification wand. The result is a large, mainstream drinkery with a pretense-free neighbourhood-bar approach, especially at night when the younger, party-hard crowd drops in for DJ dancing, live music (Thursday's reggae night is fun) or sports broadcasts—Scotland and Manchester United soccer games attract a particularly rabid following here. The handsome, saloon-look room has also been tarted up with a burnished tin ceiling, polished dark-wood bar and even a preserved sled from the old Dominion Hotel that formerly resided upstairs. A chatty side patio and a pool table round out the bar's facilities.

If you're just here for the beer, highlights include on-tap Dead Frog Lager, Rogue Dead Guy Ale and the latest seasonal tipple from Granville Island Brewing (if the Winter Ale is offered, snap it up immediately), They also have off-sale refrigerators if you need an end-of-night takeout. There's also a good whisky list, including some warming 16-year-old Bushmills malt, plus a full menu of stomach-stuffing pub grub standards. Avoid the obvious fish and chips and ask about the daily sandwich special. If it doesn't pique your appetite, head for the Cajun chicken and cheese sandwich, the highlight of the regular menu. Or drop by on a Tuesday, when a burger, fries and a beer is just $10.

Revel Room

Intimate late-night haunt with
a snug, cave-like ambience

In the early-to-mid evening, this welcoming, two-floored nook has the feel of a romantic restaurant. But as the diners slink off home, it becomes an intimate bar room and the kind of place that would be shrouded in blue smoke if smoking were allowed in Vancouver. Open to 2 AM daily (expect Sundays), the sexy Revel Room really takes off late, when it becomes a perfect respite from Gastown's more raucous drinkeries. Tucked into one of the area's heritage character buildings (it's been a butcher and shoe shop in the past), several clever features keep the old-school look alive: check out those train-car light fixtures in the washrooms, for example.

Reflecting its sophisticated but never hoity approach, there are live DJ tunes to keep things smooth on Thursday nights. The excellent drinks selection will also help keep you in the groove. BC brews from Red Truck and Russell Brewing enliven the drafts and there's an interesting array of bottled beers from Brooklyn Lager to Phillips Blue Buck Pale Ale. But cocktails are the reason for living if you're a Revel Room regular. Hunker down in a corner and drink deeply of expertly prepped treats like Jack's Canada, Sweet Caroline and the recommended Eastern Sun martini, a spicy confection of Tanqueray, lime and ginger elixir.

If you're here for the long haul, also consider a selection from the small but carefully chosen wine list (go with the Jim Jim Shiraz) accompanied by a tasting plate or two. Full dinner is available form the main menu, but after 11:30 PM a late-night nosh list of comfort dishes takes over. The mini-burgers, pulled pork sandwich and short ribs braised in cider are ever-popular but the tea-smoked duck spring rolls with tamarind dipping sauce are a standout. They're also the kind of can't-get-enough-of-'em dish that you'll happily eat until your stomach explodes. But save yourself for the end of the night: last orders here are marked with a round of fresh-baked cookies to send you home with a warm glow.

Essential tipple Eastern Sun Martini
Must-have nosh Duck Spring Rolls
Coordinates 238 Abbott Street, 604-687-4088, www.revelroom.ca

Pourhouse
Sassy homage to old saloon bars, with expert cocktails and gourmet cowboy nosh

Essential tipple Gold Fashioned
Must-have nosh Pork and Beans
Coordinates 162 Water Street, 604-568-7022, www.pourhousevancouver.com.

This new Gastown haunt seems to be of two minds about what it wants to be. On one hand, there's a cozy, laid-back bar area that quickly becomes crowded as regulars jostle for perches. While on the other side of the room, candlelit, cloth-covered tables suggest a romantic fancy restaurant. It can make for an incongruous night out, with the bar raucously hopping and diners quietly nibbling a few feet away.

Luckily, there's good reason to stick around whether you're a chomper or a barfly. Celebrating the golden age of saloon bars, the century-old, mood-lit space has some smashing heritage-chic flourishes: check out the 150-year-old French light fittings; the antique radiators fashioned into a divider between bar and dining areas; and the chunky, 120-year-old white spruce counter, hewn from a hunk of wood found on a Langley farm.

Once you've found your perch, don't be put off by the postcard-sized drinks menu. Although there seems to be only six cocktails, the expert mixologists here will create whatever you're in the mood for. Alternatively, dive in to the proscribed mini-list and its lip-smacking Gold Fashioned, made from Maker's Mark bourbon, maple syrup, d'oro, old-fashioned bitters and orange and lemon zest.

There's also a large, two-page wine selection—including unexpected bottles from Israel and Portugal—although only a few are offered by the glass. Beer-wise: ask the bartender what's available in your taste range and he'll point you to treats like Brooklyn Pennant Ale, Pilsner Urquell and Schneider-Weisse.

Reflecting the updated saloon approach, there's also an intriguing menu of elevated comfort foods, including the Pemberton beef sloppy joe sandwich and a giant "carpet bag" steak served with an oyster. Even better is the pork and beans, a hearty cassoulet-style main packed with sausage chubs and white beans. It'll fuel you up perfectly for some late-night cattle-rustling . . . or some more cocktail-sipping at the bar.

Black Frog

Unpretentious little neighbourhood bar
on a blind spot Gastown side street

Run by expat Edmontonians, this fancy-free watering hole lurks just a few feet from the blinkered Water Street pedestrians rushing past to Gastown's showier hostelries. But who needs to advertise when you have a loyal, Alberta-hugging clientele that keeps coming back for your three Big Rock drafts and those noisy screenings of Oilers's games? Of course, you don't have to be from the oil sands to quaff here. One of Vancouver's warmest little neighbourhood joints, Black Frog welcomes everyone—even if you're from Toronto.

A wood-floored patio deck (enclosed for rainy-day imbibing) dominates the frontage and is ideal for cat-like lazing in the sun on drowsy afternoons. Inside, the long bar is backed by a wall of proudly displayed kitsch including a Pee-wee Herman figurine, soccer team scarves and a full flotilla of grinning frogs. Tearing yourself away from the free-use vintage videogame console, you can park yourself on a vinyl cube in the corner, loiter around waiting for a side table or, if it's crowded, just stand around looking Albertan.

Sipping Big Rock will help your disguise but there are other brews on offer. Rare Kronenbourg Blanc is sometimes on tap but its limited availability means someone may have drunk it all before you arrive. Console yourself with a regular Kronenbourg or hit BC brews from Phillips, Okanagan Spring or Russell Brewing. The Irish triumvirate of Harp, Kilkenny and Guinness also appeals, along with bottles that include Tuborg. There's also a small wine offering plus nightcap-luring whiskies like the peaty Oban.

Comfort food with a home-cooked feel ranges from a popular baked Stilton appetizer to satisfyingly large burgers of the bulging, don't-need-to-eat-for-a-week variety. There's even a shareable Ploughman's Lunch with cheese, bread, cold cuts and pickled onions—perfect for a romantic dinner date where your eye-watering vinegar breath will be a great conversation starter. Take her mind off your onions at Friday and Saturday DJ nights or a Sunday live music event.

Essential tipple Kronenbourg Blanc
Must-have nosh Ploughman's Lunch
Coordinates 108 Cambie Street, 604-602-0527, www.theblackfrog.ca

Greedy Pig

Hipster heritage hangout with a hankering
for cured meat and southern cocktails

Essential tipple George Thorogood **Must-have nosh** Pulled Pork Sandwich **Coordinates** 307 West Cordova Street, 604-669-4991, www.thegreedypig.ca

Considering the owners hail mostly from Saskatchewan (they're not the first to escape), this narrow, cave-like drinkery feels like an old southern US saloon that's just opened up after Prohibition. That may have something to do with the menu, which leans heavily on the kind of hearty house-cured meats that vegetarians have sweaty nightmares about. Then there are the drinks: standard bar tipples are readily available, but this is the place to indulge your hankering for bourbon cocktails.

Despite looking like it's been here for decades, the high-ceilinged, brick-lined Pig is a recent Gastown addition. Perfect for winter quaffing (it can be as steamy as a barbecued hog here in the summer), its hipster crowd perches at the small high tables lining one side of the room. When not swapping tips about how best to grow their ironic sideburns, they listen to eclectic piped music ranging from muddy old blues to foot-stomping hip-hop. Local live bands can also add to the soundtrack, especially on weekends.

Drinks-wise, there are sip-worthy wines (try the Tinhorn Creek cab franc) plus on-tap Sleeman's, Red Truck and Okanagan Spring beers. And make sure you peruse the bottled selection in the chiller, archly labelled "Health Drinks." But it's the cocktails that perk up most taste buds here. Start with a Boston Sour before graduating to a Greedy Pig Manhattan with a not-so-subtle Saskatoon influence (what else can you do with those nasty berries?). Finally, slide into a body-tingling George Thorogood, made with Kentucky bourbon, Islay malt scotch and choice BC beer.

Soaking up the booze is thankfully easy here. Although the menu has some meat-free options, this is the kind of place where they spit-roast passing vegetarians. Consider a shareable cheese and butcher plate with a choice of five house-cured meats and curd treats. Or go the whole hog with bangers and hash, chicken potpie or the justifiably popular pulled pork sandwich, served with apple slaw and a piquant house barbecue sauce.

16

Steamworks

Giant, dependable brewpub favourite with
good beer and a massive food menu

Granddaddy of Vancouver's latter-day bar renaissance, the permanently popular Steamworks colonizes a labyrinthine brick-built merchant building on the edge of Gastown. It's also one of the city's few genuine brewpubs. Opened in 1995 and expanded several times, it lures a surprisingly diverse crowd of map-clutching tourists, chore-forgetting office workers and beer-loving students plus suburbanites who've hopped into town via the nearby Waterfront SkyTrain station.

It's important to choose your table carefully here— Steamworks is like several pubs in one and each area is quite different. Descend the spiral staircase to the cozy, wood-ceiling snug on comfort-hugging cold days; snag a window seat on the main floor for smashing Burrard Inlet vistas on fine days; join the nicely shaded patio for sun-kissed quaffing on balmy summer days; or drop into the slender saloon bar on the Water Street side for a comfy booth or high-chair table perch.

Wherever you sit, you'll be tempted by beers brewed on site in kettles fired by the old Gastown steam line that runs through the building. Lighter quaffers enjoy Euro-style Lions Gate Lager or seasonal-only Hefeweizen and Raspberry Frambozen, while dark tipplers dive into rich Coal Porter or Heroica Oatmeal Stout. If you're somewhere in between, the copper-coloured Signature Pale Ale and the delightfully hoppy Empress IPA will wet your whistle. Also consider weaving home with a refillable takeout growler under your arm for a hair-of-the-dog breakfast.

Line your stomach for a beery assault via the giant, multi-paged food menu. Offering comfort food classics with gourmet tweaks, you'll find blue-cheese burgers, stout-infused steak and mushroom pies, plus ever-popular pizzas and fish and chips (with their excellent beer-battered halibut). For something different, try steamed mussels or a seafood crepe, packed with salmon, prawns and scallops. Or head up the street to Steamworks' sister, the Transcontinental, a large, high-ceilinged resto-bar that's reinvented Waterfront Station's former Women's Waiting Room area.

Essential tipple Empress IPA
Must-have nosh Halibut Fish and Chips
Coordinates 375 Water Street, 604-689-2739, www.steamworks.com

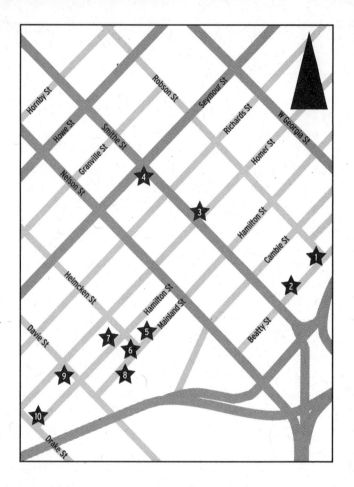

Yaletown

1. ★ Atlantic Trap & Gill
2. ★ Dix BBQ & Brewery
3. ★ Subeez
4. ★ UVA Wine Bar
5. ★ Afterglow
6. ★ Yaletown Brewing Company
7. ★ George Ultra Lounge
8. ★ Regional Tasting Lounge
9. ★ Opus Bar
10. ★ Soho Billiards

Yaletown

Created as a 19th-century freight-rail terminal lined with brick warehouses and striped with busy train tracks— workers were shipped in from the Interior town of Yale, hence the neighbourhood's historic moniker—Yaletown nightlife has come a very long way since the dodgy dive bars that once dotted the area. Most were closed long before Expo 86 rolled in to give the district a fresh start, triggering a massive regeneration that gentrified the 'hood for dot.com millionaires and urban professional yuppies.

Luckily, not everything was scrubbed away and many of the character buildings have been cleverly reinvented. In fact, some of the bars and eateries now lining the raised loading dock sidewalks of Hamilton, Homer and Mainland are among Vancouver's best haunts for a decadent night out.

Despite the concentration of collagen-stuffed lips and laser-whitened teeth, it's not all about looks here either: George is possibly the city's best cocktail bar; UVA is one of its leading wine bars; and Afterglow is a cozy cool lounge that may be the best in town for an intimate late-night tipple. And it's not all swank: two of Vancouver's best brewpubs reside in the Yaletown vicinity, so you can knock back plenty of beers while planning how to chat up the area's rich and beautiful. If you're lucky, they might be looking for a bit of rough.

Atlantic Trap & Gill
Laid-back party pub with a cheery East Coast vibe

Essential tipple Trap Lager
Must-have nosh Captain's Poutine
Coordinates 118 Robson Street, 604-688-5840, www.trapandgill.com

Newfies on the run from those cold-ass St. John's winters often spend their Vancouver hibernation time at this party-loving expat pub. Emulating a foot-stomping, wood-floored East Coast tavern better than ever since moving from its darkened former site, Trap 2.0 is the definition of a comfort-hugging, down-home drinkery. And luckily you don't have to say "aboot" to get in the door: anyone can drop in for cover-free Celtic-inspired live music on Thursdays and Saturdays, but you'll be warmly welcomed into the fold whichever day you roll in.

Perhaps the biggest improvement over the old location is the patio, which almost doubles the size of the bar's drinking area. It's an ideal summer-evening haunt for a plate of heaping seafood and a few pitchers of beer with chatty mates at a large communal table. Inside—which feels as alfresco as the patio when the garage-style doors are flung open—you'll be rubbing shoulders with an eclectic mix of easterners, old lags and a large contingent of students and twentysomethings enjoying a raucous group night out.

While some of them might be sipping wine, the majority are here for the beer. Steer away from the giant Kokanee tap on the bar (even if it's on special) and consider draft Alexander Keith's IPA, all the way from Halifax. Guinness, Stella Artois and three Granville Island Brewing tipples round out the familiar selection. Alternatively, go for the Trap Lager: Russell Brewing Lager in disguise, it's often on special and slides down easier than a warm bowl of clam chowder.

Speaking of which, the Trap's nosh—clearly designed to lag stomachs for a season of hardy trawler work—is suitably dominated by seafood. The aforementioned clam chowder is worth a punt, but variations include the excellent chunky seafood chowder (served with biscuits) and the scarily calorific Captain's Poutine (fries topped with battered cod and chowder). It's a great final meal to request before you hit the electric chair.

Dix BBQ & Brewery

Comfy trad bar with great-value house-brewed
beers and hearty Southern-style grub

One of the city's few genuine brewpubs, the off-the-beaten-path Dix is a relaxed, pretense-free watering hole for those tired of the overly glamorous Yaletown scene: there aren't many regulars here with yapping chihuahuas in their handbags, for example. An instantly warming combination of dark-wood counters, battered chairs, twin pool tables and a tavern-style mosaic floor topped with discarded peanut shells, it's hard to imagine a better-looking trad boozer, especially when you spot the huge steel beer vats nestled behind glass panels. They dominate the room like an altar dedicated to booze.

Worship from afar or dive right in to find your fave brew—the great beer prices here encourage plenty of experimental sampling. Popular suds include a nicely hopped IPA and a lighter, lager-style Game Day Pilsner that's easy to drink in quantity (which, of course, is exactly what happens when Canucks or BC Lions games flicker to life on the bar's TVs). Connoisseurs also like straying to the dark side. Dix's darker ales—discounted by $1 on Monday nights—are ever-changing but often include a tasty German-style dark lager, along with seasonal stouts and heady winter tipples. True beer nuts should save themselves for Thursdays when a guest cask is cracked open for the night (arrive at 5 PM to be sure of a taste).

But it's not just about beer at Dix. The Southern-style food menu is a revelation here and it's worth rolling in for even if you're a die-hard teetotaler. Bring your appetite for huge, carnivore-pleasing meals like barbecued meatloaf, velvet-soft brisket sandwiches or a mess of St. Louis side ribs, all slow-prepared in an apple wood–fuelled oven. Side orders of cornbread and mashed potatoes should fill you up for a week. If you don't want to stuff your beer belly with carbs, though, the excellent jambalaya is recommended. It's bursting with sausage, shrimp and pulled chicken goodness.

Essential tipple Game Day Pilsner
Must-have nosh Jambalaya
Coordinates 871 Beatty Street, 604-682-2739, www.drinkfreshbeer.com

Subeez

Huge and seductive party cave
that's ideal for a flirty night out

Essential tipple Pom Surprise

Must-have nosh Chicken and Brie Sandwich

Coordinates 891 Homer Street, 604-687-6107, www.subeez.com

The high walls are dripping with oddball art while the cavernous, mood-lit interior is studded with giant candles plumed with hardened wax. Dominating the corner of Homer and Smithe streets, Subeez is one of the city's most original bars and it manages to be both enormous and intimate at the same time. Echoing the clamorous watering holes of Montreal (if it suddenly appeared on Boulevard Saint-Laurent, no one would bat an eyelid), this is a great spot for late-night carousing. You'll find a flirty crowd of young barflies mixing it up with an older crew lured by the impressive drinks selection ... or just hiding in the darkened corners enjoying a romantic dinner.

Friday and Saturday DJ nights are the best times to party here. Huddle around the circular bar and rub shoulders with your cohorts (it'll be too noisy to chat) or take a respite from the vibe on a blue vinyl banquette or an outside patio bench away from the throbbing revelry. Wherever you grind to a halt, make some time to peruse the drinks array. Impressive beers like Crannóg Organic Bitter, Storm Scottish Ale or the scarily strong Maudite from Quebec (plus the rare Big Rock Rock Creek Cider) are available, but it's the naughty martinis and other cocktails that slake most thirsts here.

All the classics and more are available but the Pom Surprise (muddied cucumber and gin with pomegranate syrup and fresh lime juice) is a highlight. There's also a surprisingly good wine selection. Dominated by BC, it includes select international treats like France's Red Bicyclette Pinot Noir.

Elevated above standard bar fare, the food menu has plenty of tempting highlights. In fact, coming here on a quieter night can make for a cozy dinner date. Shareables like calamari or crab cakes are popular and there are several worthwhile pasta and gourmet burger dishes. But the best meal here is the chicken and brie sandwich ... especially if coupled with a side order of addictive Cajun yam fries.

UVA Wine Bar
Sassy wine nook with a warm, snob-free ambience

Radically transforming a corner of the infamous old Dufferin Pub site, this is one of the few Vancouver boîtes that truly deserve its "wine bar" label. And that's mostly due to resident sommelier and waxed-moustache aficionado Sebastien Le Goff, who's helped foster an approach that's both wine-appreciative and snob-free. Duck in for a quick quaff and you'll find yourself still there several hours later, with a long, lip-smacking list of empty glasses to your name.

Retaining the mosaic floors and high ceilings of the century-old Moda Hotel building and jazzing them up with mod touches like white vinyl easy chairs, round marble tables and chrome cluster light fittings, the sleek little space is dominated by its curving, red-cushioned bar. This corner counter is the ideal spot to park yourself and, if it's quiet enough, partake of a few winey tips directly from the friendly maestro himself.

Instead of a bewildering multi-page menu, there's a manageable four-page array here focusing on French, Italian, US and New Zealand offerings, plus some interesting BC tipples: the grapefruity Joie Riesling from the Okanagan hits the spot nicely, for example. Keep in mind that fewer than half the wines are available by the glass, so you'll have to restrict your tastings . . . or just move on to the cocktails. The Perfect Manhattan really is (and it's a reminder that not many bars in the city can nail it this well), but consider the excellent Earl Grey Martini if you want to try something satisfyingly different.

The food is all about tasting plates at UVA, with interesting tidbits like sardine bruschetta and the recommended zucchini flowers stuffed with goat cheese. There's also a good choice of cured charcuterie and tasty artisan cheeses to accompany your sipping marathon—if you're lucky, the sharp, richly veined gorgonzola will be available. Open to 2 AM most evenings, your fellow late-night tipplers will often be staff from other bars dropping by for a gossipy, end-of-session wind-down.

Essential tipple Earl Grey Martini
Must-have nosh Zucchini Flowers Stuffed with Goat Cheese
Coordinates 900 Seymour Street, 604-632-9560, www.uvawinebar.ca

Afterglow

Sexy little lounge that feels far from
the madding Yaletown crowds

Essential tipple You Glow Girl

Must-have nosh Scallops and Bacon Satay

Coordinates 1079 Mainland Street, 604-602-0835, www.glowbalgrill.com

Where in-the-know-locals tired of the competitive hordes cramming Yaletown's usual bar suspects like to hang out, this cozy den is an ideal late-night chill spot. Little more than a mood-lit nest of comfy couches, scatter cushions and mod side tables, it still manages to be effortlessly cool and seductive—the '60s lampshades, whitewashed brickwork and pink silhouettes snaking the walls certainly help.

Although it's located behind the ever-busy, often noisy Glowbal Restaurant, this space is surprisingly calm and intimate. And it's a great spot to make some new Yaletown buddies: you'll be squeezed so close to the next group on your couch that impromptu chats, casual flirting or even an unplanned pregnancy are almost inevitable.

Mirroring the room's tiny stature, there's a small but well-formed drinks menu here focused on cocktails and martinis. Highlights include the naughty Black Cherry Mojito and the recommended You Glow Girl, concocted from Plymouth Gin, sour apple and white grape juice. Fairly standard bottled import and domestic beers are also offered—they sadly don't carry those uber-strong Quebec Unibroues any more—and the wine selection from the adjoining restaurant is fully available back here.

Starving quaffers should head to Glowbal for a full dinner choice but if you're just looking for some tasty snacks to accompany your tipple, Afterglow's lip-smacking satay sticks are the way to go. A house specialty, they include varieties like Creole-crusted oyster and the recommended scallops wrapped in bacon. If you're in for a languid night of group indulgence, consider a platter of several different satays or add a side dish of Kobe meatballs or black truffle popcorn. And if you're on a romantic night out, share a Toblerone chocolate fondue—just make sure you don't spill it on your pricey designer togs.

Yaletown Brewing Company

Convivial brick-lined bar with lip-smacking
house brews and gourmet grub

A recent makeover has transformed the larger restaurant side of this Yaletown anchor into a slick Milestones clone. But, mercifully, the narrow, brick-lined pub side has been spruced up without affecting its beloved barroom chops. You'll still find the huge stone-look hearth, well-used back-of-the-room pool tables and that combination of inside high perches plus a small alfresco patio that's ideal for eyeing Yaletown's beautiful people. But the refurb hasn't only touched the restaurant: the bar's wood-beamed ceiling now includes spent beer kegs deployed as evocative lampshades. (Don't try this at home).

A clamorous corridor of noisy quaffers on weekends (expect to overhear conversations about stock options and sports cars), this popular brewpub—check the brimming tanks at the back—serves some lip-smacking house brews. The malty Downtown Brown and well-hopped Nagila Pale Ale are popular but the dark, silky-smooth Warehouse Stout is recommended. Drop by at 4 PM on Thursdays when they tap a special cask (then scamper over to Dix, where they do the same at 5 PM). Reflecting its Yaletown audience, it's not just about the beer here, of course. There's a gratifying large wine array, impressively all sourced from BC, plus a dizzying menu of cocktails to toast your latest high-finance triumph.

The gourmet-flecked food selection has been revamped along with the building. Old faves remain (remove pizza from the menu here and there'd be a riot), while new additions include Japanese-style wild salmon and beef tenderloin stroganoff. While these dishes better suit the adjoining restaurant area, visitors on this side of the fence are more likely to slide down the pizza route. Far from your average dog-eared pepperoni pie, the best option here is the delectable duck leg, toasted walnut and blue cheese variety.

Essential tipple Warehouse Stout
Must-have nosh Duck Pizza
Coordinates 1111 Mainland Street, 604-681-2739, www.drinkfreshbeer.com

George Ultra Lounge

Seductive lounge room with possibly
the city's best cocktails

Essential tipple Old Fashioned

Must-have nosh Pork Buns

Coordinates 1137 Hamilton Street, 604-628-5555, www.georgelounge.com

Yaletown's leading lounge, this clubby, elbow-shaped drinkery is the ideal spot to pretend you're a visiting young Internet millionaire with a yacht parked at Quayside Marina. In summer, slide onto the mod-look patio to bask in the late-evening sun or duck inside and tuck yourself into the lip-shaped red booth in the corner. Of course, there are other tables, but standing is de rigueur here—especially on Wednesdays and Thursdays when thumping DJs take over and on weekends when the place is jam-packed with dressed-to-kill Yaletown glitterati.

Twinned with Brix (the resto-wine bar is up the stairs at the back), George is all about fine cocktails. But unlike other bars claiming similar chops, this place really knows what it's talking about, hosting some of Vancouver's most renowned mixologists. Look past the spirally glass Brillo-pad thing hanging from the ceiling and behind the bar you'll spot a fruit-, spice- and veggie-topped table that might be more at home in a kitchen. In fact, this is where the fresh cocktail ingredients are prepped each night.

Fusing classics and hot contemporary mixes, you'll find a tempting selection of old and new tipples on offer. There are perfectly executed Manhattans, Mint Juleps and Tom Collins, but you'll also find house signatures like the tall 1903 Collins of BC cherry–infused gin with maraschino liqueur, fresh lemon and violet soda. There's also an intriguing mini-list of five cocktails from bars around the world plus a premium menu of extra specials: celebrate those new stock options with a $50 XO Mint Julep built on the famed Hennessy cognac. If you only have one drink here, though, make it the classic Old Fashioned: it never fails to hit home.

Food-wise, tasting plates are the way to go at George with a small array of lip-smacking treats like Kobe beef burgers, curried shrimp frites and a decidedly naughty chocolate trio dessert. It's the handmade spring rolls and stuffed pork buns that attract most snackers, though. They might help sober you up before you have to remember where you parked the boat.

Regional Tasting Lounge

Intimate taste tripper with an ever-changing
drink-and-dine array

Press your face to the smoked-glass exterior like a Victorian
street urchin and peer in at one of the city's best new drink-
and-dine tapas joints. Then, since you can't suck the nosh
off the tables through the windows (believe me, I've tried),
nip inside for an evening of dedicated taste tripping. You'll
find an intimate, candlelit room studded with mod vinyl
chairs and glossy, dark wood tables that's underscored by
a sophisticated but friendly approach. It invites you to
sit back, forget about work and gorge like a bacchanalian
awakening from hibernation.

Never resting on its menu laurels, the "regional" part
of the moniker here means that food and drink selections
change every three months. They focus on three areas: one
is always BC, while the others have included Spain, Greece,
Italy, etc. The approach delivers an always-intriguing array
of tipples and tasting plates from around the world, although
I'm still waiting for the Brit tapas menu showcasing fish
fingers, baked beans and spotted dick (don't ask).

There's a wine bar approach to grape-based imbibing
here—they have one of those swanky Enomatic serving
machines—with many available by the full glass or in
2.5oz tasting servings. In contrast, the cocktail menu stays
constant, but there are plans to add regional specials in
the future. The tiny back bar serves a full array of cocktail
classics plus a few contemporary twists—try the delightful
Pistachio Sour of woody grappa, Amontillado sherry,
pistachio paste, lime juice and orange blossom water.

While the selection of sharing plates you won't want
to share is always changing, there are usually places on
the menu for Berkshire pork belly and the unmissable
oak barrel house-smoked duck magret. And don't worry if
your date has stood you up: head to the room's back corner
and choose a foodie tome from the bookcase to keep you
company. Don't try taking the *Dickens Digest*, though: it'll
release the mechanism and swing the bookcase open to
reveal a secret, sofa-lined den hidden behind.

Essential tipple Pistachio Sour
Must-have nosh House-smoked Duck Magret
Coordinates 1130 Mainland Street, 604-638-1550, www.rtl

Opus Bar

Swish scenester lounge fuelled by great
cocktails and celebrity sightings

Essential tipple Opus 97
Must-have nosh Pecorino Fries
Coordinates 350 Davie Street, 604-642-0557, www.opusbar.ca

My server could neither confirm nor deny that Harrison Ford and Robert De Niro once rolled in here together for a beer, but she did mention that Zac Efron (surely the new De Niro) had recently dropped by. And then there was Chris Rock, Britney Spears and lantern-jawed vampire Robert Pattinson. The Opus Hotel has some rivals in the local boutique sleepover stakes, but its bar remains a top spot for visiting celebs and their shiny-eyed hangers-on

Divided between a tiny Parisian bar adorned with a stained-glass ceiling and an aesthetically opposite lobby lounge of theatrical thrones and gilded tables, DJ-driven weekend nights here are an exercise in how the other half looks. You'll spot more pricey designer outfits, Louis Vuitton purses and young women in cleavage-promoting dresses than you ever thought possible. They're here to have a flirty good time, and perhaps snare that rich celeb or stockbroker that might be passing through.

There's a full array of dangerously addictive cocktails to keep you company, including some good Bellinis and old-school Manhattans. But if you go for the Opus 97, you'll fit right in. Named after the hotel's original room count (there are now 96), it's concocted from Belvedere Pomarancza vodka, Alize Gold Passion and blood orange juice. After a couple, you'll be bragging about your Hollywood contacts and promising movie roles to anyone who'll listen. There's also a good three-page array of wines, plus a surprisingly extensive whisky choice that includes seven from the malt-sodden Isle of Islay.

Take a booze break with a full meal from the hotel's Elixir restaurant menu or nibble on tempting gourmet tapas like petit burgers or the daily-changing O Pizza. Even better are the decadent Pecorino fries, with cheese, truffle oil and garlic aioli. Don't miss the downstairs washrooms either: their in-wall video screens broadcast from the lounge so you can plan your next conquest. And that swishing beaded curtain by the door? It's for naughty peeking into the adjoining washroom where the ladies will be reapplying their war paint.

Soho Billiards

Atmospheric edge-of-Yaletown haunt
with a laid-back, late-night feel

Keep walking west on Hamilton. Pass the chi-chi restaurants. Pass the swanky lounges. Then go a little further. Right at the end of the 1200-block—Siberia in Yaletown terms—you'll find the kind of fancy-free, old-school haunt that stands out in this 'hood like a pair of grubby Wranglers in a pile of pristine Calvin Kleins. And that's exactly what makes it special. Welcome to Soho Billiards, a funky and evocatively shady pool hall where you don't have to knock the balls around to have a good time.

A surprisingly diverse crowd of chilling-out Yaletownites, chatty ESL students and in-the-know regulars drop by to hit one of the eight mood-lit tables at the back of the room here. But even better is the front-of-house bar area that lures quaffers with absolutely no intention of stroking the baize (that's not a naughty euphemism). Step up to the lounge space and snag one of the mismatched wooden dining tables or just sink into the scuffed leather couch that looks capable of swallowing a small ESL student whole. On sunny days, there's even a little patio area that's ideal for leering like a blue-collar hick at the passing Yaletown ladies.

Amidst a cozy interior of heritage advertising signs and some edgy local art, there's a hearty array of fairly standard beers. Not really a place for cocktails—they'll make 'em but this isn't George Ultra Lounge—the highlight drafts include Sleeman Honey Brown, Okanagan Spring 1516 and the recommended Shaftebury Coastal Cream Ale. Bottle-wise, you'll find predictable suspects like Sol, Moosehead and Stella Artois.

And if you need a food break between games, it's all about diet-abandoning pub grub. Check the chalkboard above the bar for regular specials on options like nachos, chicken strips and burger sandwiches. Then go for the tasty and justifiably popular tuna melt, the best thing on the list.

Essential tipple Shaftebury Coastal Cream Ale
Must-have nosh Tuna Melt
Coordinates 1283 Hamilton Street, 604-688-1180, www.sohocafe.ca

Drink: best bars for . . .

BC microbrews
Alibi Room, 6
Backstage Lounge, 123
St. Augustine's, 87

Brewpub beer
Dix BBQ & Brewery, 21
Steamworks, 17
Yaletown Brewing
  Company, 25

Bottled beer selection
Alibi Room, 6
Fringe Café, 132
Six Acres, 11

Belgian beer
Chambar, 59
Six Acres, 11
Stella's, 93 & 111

Budget boozing
Cambie, 76
Granville Island
  Brewing Taproom, 120
Pat's Pub, 81

Cask ale events
St. Augustine's, 87
Whip, 99
Yaletown Brewing
  Company, 25

Cocktails
Cascade Room, 103
Diamond, 7
George Ultra Lounge, 26

Whisky
Bacchus Lounge, 53
Habit Lounge, 102
Irish Heather, 9

Wine
Au Petit Chavignol, 82
Salt Tasting Room, 10
UVA Wine Bar, 23

Dine: best bars for . . .

Gastropub dishes
Cascade Room, 103
Irish Heather, 9
Three Lions Café, 101

Tapas
Bin 941, 71
Guu with Garlic, 65
Regional Tasting
  Lounge, 27

Cheese & charcuterie
Au Petit Chavignol, 82
Irish Heather, 9
Salt Tasting Room, 10

Heaping pub grub
Atlantic Trap & Gill, 20
Dix BBQ & Brewery, 21
Falconetti's, 89

Gourmet comfort food
Alibi Room, 6
Corduroy, 128
Narrow Lounge, 98

Seafood
Cardero's, 63
Galley Patio & Grill, 137
O Lounge, 49

Vegetarian options
Foundation, 100
Fringe Café, 132
Nevermind, 135

Budget dining
Metropole, 78
Pat's Pub, 81
Railway Club, 55

Late-night noshing
Bin 941, 71
Corduroy, 128
Revel Room, 13

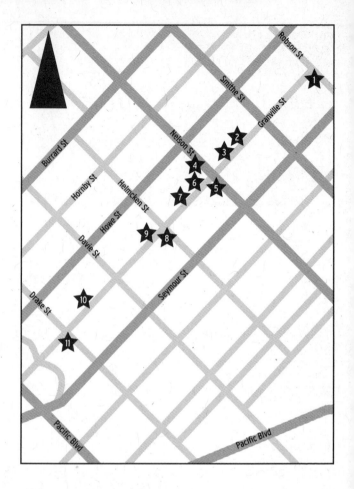

Granville Strip

★ Lennox Pub
★ Granville Room
★ Lux at Caprice
★ Loose Moose
★ Doolin's Irish Pub
★ Whineos
★ Johnnie Fox's Irish Snug
★ Edge Lounge
★ Sip Resto Lounge
★ Morrissey Irish House
★ Yale

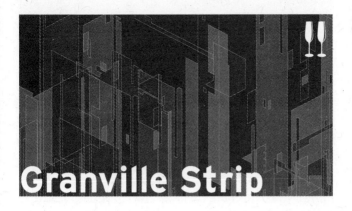

Granville Strip

Formerly a nightlife wonderland of twinkling 1950s neon signalling a plethora of bars, restaurants, theatres and show lounges where Vancouverites kicked back after a long working week, the Strip—from Robson to the bridge—stumbled like an old drunk into painful decline in the 1970s. Many of the best joints flicked the switches on their signage for the last time, only to be replaced by an ever-changing menu of inferior haunts. By the turn of the new century, things began changing with better spots opening alongside the rubbish ones and a return to the long-abandoned policy of encouraging nightlife neon.

With a welcome makeover triggered by Canada Line construction, the Strip is poised to return to its glory days. On weekends, you'll find a mostly under-25 party crowd (many in from the suburbs for their binge-drinking big night out) dressed in shiny nightclub togs and determined to chug, dance and chat each other up as if their lives depended on it. During the week, it's considerably less raucous and you'll be able to check out the bars without feeling like you're trapped in a drunken, open-air vomitorium. You'll find a wide array of options to chose from, including the pub-style Lennox and Doolin's; the lounge-swank Lux and Edge; and the Yale, a cavernous old gal with a kickin' live blues roster.

Lennox Pub

Trad-style meeting-place boozer
on the end of the Strip

Essential tipple Leffe

Must-have nosh Irish Stew

Coordinates 800 Granville Street, 604-408-0881

Granville Street's least pretentious bar, the brightly lit, wood-lined Lennox has become comfortably worn in recent years, giving it the feel of an old-school pub that's been here far longer than it has. A popular meeting place for partiers about to launch into a night of raucous shenanigans in nearby clubs, it attracts a diverse crowd of miniskirted youngsters, older barflies who hate the Strip's loungier bars and curious tourists reassured by the no-surprises look of the place.

While these groups couldn't be more different, all are united on game nights when Canucks battles flicker to life on TVs above the bar. But even when there's no hockey, the narrow Lennox can be noisy, especially on weekends when the place is heaving with animated conversation and tables are as rare as a glass of draft nachos. Try for a seat at the sad little patio outside or decamp to the hidden snug area upstairs at the back. Alternatively, just drop in during the week when it's much quieter.

You'll encounter a good selection of 15 drafts, including standouts Harp, Strongbow and Big Rock Grasshopper. Even better is the tasty triumvirate of Belgian taps comprising Hoegaarden, Stella Artois and the strong but recommended Leffe. Be aware that slightly higher Strip prices are in operation—Guinness, for example, costs $7.50. If you just need some Dutch courage before hitting the area's dance floors, consider the whiskies winking at you from the high shelf behind the bar. Sadly they won't let you ride on the sliding ladder attached to it.

Lennox food is of the typical pub grub variety, with a few highlights. Alongside the usual burger suspects, you'll find a Tandoori chicken version, while nestled in the salad offerings is a popular chicken and avocado variety. And even though it's not a traditional Irish bar (it's actually more like the slightly confused offspring of Gaelic and Belgian parents), the pub's best chow is a hearty Irish stew, made with chunks of tender lamb.

Granville Room
Flirty black-decored bar where your
best chat-up lines are expected

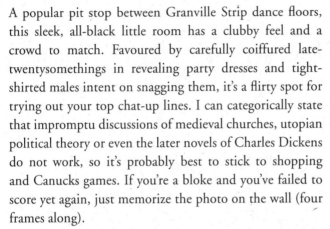

Essential tipple Mint Julep
Must-have nosh Yam Frites
Coordinates 957 Granville Street, 604-633-0056, www.dhmbars.ca

A popular pit stop between Granville Strip dance floors, this sleek, all-black little room has a clubby feel and a crowd to match. Favoured by carefully coiffured late-twentysomethings in revealing party dresses and tight-shirted males intent on snagging them, it's a flirty spot for trying out your top chat-up lines. I can categorically state that impromptu discussions of medieval churches, utopian political theory or even the later novels of Charles Dickens do not work, so it's probably best to stick to shopping and Canucks games. If you're a bloke and you've failed to score yet again, just memorize the photo on the wall (four frames along).

Alternatively, you can console yourself with a drink, although it's best not to get too wasted or you might try hitting on the chair next to you. Since the wall of booze behind the bar will be staring at you, experiment with an impressive bottled array that includes Anchor Steam, Red Stripe and Asahi Super Dry (draft Rogue Dead Guy Ale is additionally available). There's also a good cocktail menu with two pages of treats fusing both classic and contemporary approaches—Mint Juleps are justifiably popular here but the Strawberry Cup of Pimms, muddled strawbs, lemon juice, orange juice and ginger ale is an ideal offering to the lady of your choice.

If it doesn't work, hit one of the three varieties of absinthe or indulge in some compensatory comfort eating. Mains are available (steak is popular and the miso-marinated halibut is recommended) but small plates are the way to go here. Those skinny yam frites with smoked garlic mayo really hit the spot, but spring rolls, Salt Spring mussels and soy-cured salmon are also good additions. And make sure you check the specials: since this is primarily a late-night haunt (open to 2 AM every evening), there are some good deals to entice the off-peak crowd, including two-for-one small plates between 4 PM and 7 PM daily.

Lux at Caprice

Swanky Strip respite for well-dressed clubbers

Essential tipple Stone Lotus
Must-have nosh Trio of Mini-burgers
Coordinates 965 Granville Street, 604-685-3189, www.luxatcaprice.com

A sleek lounge pit stop where club nuts from the on-site and area dance floors refuel or chill with their new-found beaus, this bar has been radically transformed from its former brooding, all-back interior. The light new look combines curlicue-patterned wallpaper with bordello-black chandeliers, Friesian-hide sofas and a glowing pink bar backdrop. Among its clutch of candlelit mod tables, there's a single circular red vinyl booth that's the most sought-after seat in the house: stay here all night and you can expect green-eyed imbibers to eye you enviously for the duration.

A dressier young crowd than the usual Granville Strip haunts—the drinkers here are generally togged up for flirtatious clubbing—the main libation attractions are on the cocktail menu. Among the 10 sip-worthy treats (from Bellinis to Furo-Gamas) is the recommended Stone Lotus of Tanqueray, sake, cucumber, citrus and cinnamon. It slides down like a melting pat of butter on an angled mirror. A larger-than-expected 30-plus array of mostly New World wines, about half of them available by the glass, adds to the liquid temptations.

Three draughts (Heineken, Guinness and Rickards White) aim to keep the beer drinkers happy, but there's also a good list of bottled brews including Carlsberg, Peroni, Red Stripe and Anchor Steam. And if, like me, you're one of those people who really needs to be massively drunk to hit the dance floor, the ultra-strong Maudite will have you either boogying like a demented demon or cooling your throbbing head on the sidewalk outside (you won't be the only one).

If you need more than booze to fuel your merry jigging, Lux offers a few entrees that are comparatively well priced for the Strip (try the roasted lamb). Even better is the longer list of tapas, priced at $10 per plate or $25 for three. The mango chicken, crab lollipops and pizza-like foccacia flatbreads are popular but the trio of mini-burgers is the way to go. Don't plan to share or there'll be a big fight over this tuna, sirloin beef and Italian chicken slider plate.

Loose Moose

Grubby party pub offering a rocking good time

Vying with nearby El Furniture Warehouse as the grungy highlight of the Strip's bar offerings—think sticky tables, gum-studded carpets and a thumping soundtrack—this fancy-free little spot is just off the main drag on Nelson. It's favoured by party-hard locals and those heavy drinkers in from the suburbs aiming to blot out all memory of their lives back in Whalley. Tame by day, the bleary-eyed Moose likes to get down at night: she's open to 2 AM and shouts her intent on the mural outside: "We rock eight days a week."

On balmy nights, grab a perch at the open roll-up front window and you'll be perfectly positioned to hoot and holler at passersby. Alternatively, slouch over the small bar inside or try for one of the sought-after back tables, each illuminated by a sawn-off beer bottle serving as a lampshade. They make for great reading lamps, but this is not the kind of place to hunker down in a corner with a small sherry and a Sartre paperback, although it would be entertaining to watch someone try.

Beer-wise, there are some worthwhile brews alongside the Kokanee pitchers. Draft Sleeman, Okanagan Spring and Alexander Keith's are available and there are bottles of Red Stripe, Pabst Blue Ribbon and even Boston's Samuel Adams Lager to keep things interesting—check the daily specials before selecting. You can also head down the slippery vodka slope with a few Mike's Hard coolers. Don't blame me if you wake up the next morning in an amnesiac haze with your Sartre book inserted where the sun don't shine.

The Loose Moose food menu includes a few unexpected entrees like jambalaya, but it's the simpler pub grub that appears on most tables. The blackened chicken burger is justly popular, while the piled-high nacho plate is great for a rabidly peckish huddle of sociable drinkers. If you're really starving, hit the Moose Platter, a shareable grease-fest of wings, strips, fries, et al.

Essential tipple Samuel Adams Lager Must-have nosh Blackened Chicken Burger Coordinates 724 Nelson Street, 604-633-1002, www.loosemoosevancouver.com

Doolin's Irish Pub
Vancouver's best-looking Emerald Isle tavern

Essential tipple Murphy's Must-have nosh Crab Cheddar Melt Coordinates 654 Nelson Street, 604-605-4343, www.doolins.ca

While most North American Irish pubs look about as authentic as a plastic shillelagh, Doolin's fits the bill far better than most, although you wouldn't know it from outside. Push through the heavy door and you're suddenly cocooned in a chunky wood-beamed interior that's studded with stained glass, worn dartboards, scuffed floorboards and wonky tables of all shapes and sizes. It's just the kind of cavernous, old-school tavern still found on the main streets of Cork and Galway.

A clamorous party joint on weekends—the Strip is just a couple of steps away after all—the best seats here are up a couple of steps behind the bar, where you'll find a pair of traditional, almost fully enclosed private tables perfect for a night of group carousing. You'll still be able to hear the nightly music offerings percolating through the room (Thursday there's a Newfie-style Celtic band, weekends are for DJs and the rest of the week is a solitary guitar guy in the corner) but you'll also feel like you're having your own little party.

While the 18 on-tap brews here—proper 20oz pint servings—range up to $7.25, there's always a well-priced daily special (it's Guinness on Mondays). And if you're really on a tight budget, consider dressing up for the first Thursday of every month when kilt-wearers receive a free pint. Most Irish hostelries stick to the usual Guinness-Harp-Kilkenny triumvirate, but Doolin's also pours creamy Caffrey's and Murphy's, a stout alternative to Guinness. Both are rare drafts in Vancouver and the latter is especially worth a try.

There's also a giant pub grub selection to line your stomach, ranging from standards like shepherd's pie and lamb stew to less familiar "Irish fare" like barbecued pulled pork sandwiches and coconut chicken curry. But for something a little different, go for the tasty crab cheddar melt served with avocado on an Irish crumpet. It's just the kind of exotic nosh that would be hailed as a major gourmet treat in the potato-loving bars of the motherland.

Whineos

Comfy bohemian-look wine bar with tasty tapas menu

The best decor of any bar on the Strip, the interior of the ultra-narrow Whineos is lined with flock-wallpaper sections, oddball local artworks, a zebra skin that's escaped from its frame and a row of wine-bottle lampshades hanging over the small back bar. There's also a side snug with closable bookcase doors (it's known as the Scooby Doo Room) and a hidden, ladder-accessed mezzanine that looks perfect for crashing if you drink too much.

Grab a perch at one of the dark-wood candlelit high tables and you'll be joining a buzzing, chatty crowd that's often slightly older (think 25 to 35) than many of the area's other watering holes—except on Tuesdays, when giddy youngsters and fresh-faced students line up to guzzle $7.50 pitcher specials as if there's no uni the next day.

Ostensibly a wine bar—although the name, spelled differently, means alcoholic in my UK lexicon—Whineos actually serves a greater volume of playful cocktails like She-Hulk and Cabo Call-Girl. Even better is the Sexual Tension of peach schnapps, Absolut Pear, Triple Sec, cranberry juice and orange juice. And while beer-wise, there's not much to excite (Sol, Stella, Becks, etc.), wine lovers will find the Strip's best bottle selection. There are 20 mostly well-priced offerings available by the glass, around half from BC wineries like Sandhill, Stags Head and Blasted Church. Additional bottle-only selections round out the list.

You can pair your drink with a full entree (the crispy potato-wrapped salmon is good) or spilt a few fusion tapas at your table. Larger "fork tapas" include perogies, Bombay calamari and mushroom risotto cakes, while the smaller "finger tapas" centre on tasty Cajun tuna crisps, open-faced sliders and the justifiably popular tempura tuna roll. If you're on the wine road, consider the Deconstructed Pizza, a tasty plate of flat bread served with scoopable toppings like sliced mozzarella, olive tapenade, artichoke salsa, grilled sausage and tomato-parmesan marinara.

Essential tipple Sexual Tension
Must-have nosh Deconstructed Pizza
Coordinates 1017 Granville Street, 604-669-9463, www.whineos.com

Johnnie Fox's Irish Snug

A comfy trad bar in the heart of the
Granville Strip mayhem

Essential tipple Poor Man's Black Velvet **Must-have nosh** Yorkies **Coordinates** 1033 Granville Street, 604-685-4946, www.johnniefox.ca

One swift stride while you're looking the other way and you'll pass this tiny hole-in-the-wall pub without even noticing it. But if you're looking for an unassuming salt-of-the-earth bar where you can escape from the party-hard Granville Strip, retrace your steps and nip through the red door. You'll find a narrow, convivial drinkery that mercifully doesn't batter you over the head with that Irish theme bar approach (except on St. Patrick's Day, of course, when the place is crawling with shillelagh-wielding leprechauns).

Perching at the little bar is *de rigueur* for the late-twenties males who drink here every day, but the best seats are at the back where a step-up side platform of small tables faces a much sought-after pairing of wood and glass-enclosed booths. If they're free, snag one and stay the night. The bar's jumbled decor mixes a half-hearted Irish aesthetic—including the obligatory Guinness mirror—with an oddball menagerie of dusty, moth-eaten stuffed ducks and bear heads. You'll also spot some wall-mounted rugby and soccer memorabilia, indicating that the TVs here are usually tuned to sports.

For drinks, the usual hat trick of Irish brews is on offer, plus a surprisingly large array of "mixed drafts" that include shandy, snakebite, and lager and lime. For a change of taste, try the smooth Poor Man's Black Velvet, a tasty fusion of Guinness and Strongbow. A smattering of mainly BC wines and the usual whisky suspects round out the libations list.

Food-wise, all the usual pub grub standards are on the menu: you could offer duck confit and Chilean sea bass here but burgers would still be the top seller. Indeed, the bulging Johnnie Fox Burger is the most popular dish, but you should consider a Yorkies appetizer instead. It's a Yorkshire pudding stuffed with roast beef and brimming with gravy. If you're still hungry after that, you can rediscover your Irish roots with bangers and colcannon mash. Good fuel for the dance floors nearby.

Edge Lounge

Slick older-crowd oasis with a rare patio attraction

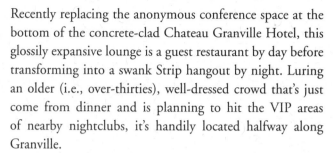

Recently replacing the anonymous conference space at the bottom of the concrete-clad Chateau Granville Hotel, this glossily expansive lounge is a guest restaurant by day before transforming into a swank Strip hangout by night. Luring an older (i.e., over-thirties), well-dressed crowd that's just come from dinner and is planning to hit the VIP areas of nearby nightclubs, it's handily located halfway along Granville.

The mood-lit aesthetic here is typical West Coast cool, complete with polished hardwood floors, a heavy granite bar and that low-slung mod seating beloved of Yaletown expats, one of the lounge's main audiences. But it's not just about slick interiors here. The Edge also offers the Strip's only real patio, a clumsily hedged-in corner of Granville and Helmcken that's nevertheless a welcome oasis for cool summertime quaffing.

It's an ideal spot for an ice-cold draft Red Truck Lager or a glistening bottle of chilled Anchor Steam. Of course, the clientele here is often into slightly more sophisticated libations: the dangerously seductive Edge Martini, concocted from espresso vodka, Jägermeister and chocolate, slips down like liquid velvet and may have you forgetting exactly which nightclub you're supposed to be weaving to next. A boutique array of martinis, additional cocktails and mostly New World wines—Sandhill Pinot Gris is recommended for summer sipping—rounds out the selection.

There's also a cut-above-average late-night food menu to keep you occupied. Clever shareables include a charcuterie plate of meats and local cheeses, as well as some finger-licking salt-and-pepper-crusted chicken lollipops, served with a piquant chili sauce. The four flatbread pizza varieties are also excellent, especially the duck sausage, red cabbage and Provolone option—you'll order it to share and then end up hogging the whole thing. Heartier appetites should instead head for the decadent mac and cheese, blended with black truffles.

Essential tipple Edge Martini
Must-have nosh Duck Sausage Flatbread Pizza
Coordinates 1100 Granville Street, 604-681-3343, www.theedgeongranville.com

Sip Resto Lounge

Casual, mood-lit bar with an intriguing
booze-based food menu

Essential tipple Diablo **Must-have nosh** Prawn and Crab Cakes **Coordinates** 1117 Granville Street, 604-687-7474, www.siplounge.com

While there's an older, more Yaletowny crowd at the upstairs
Refinery, the ground-level Sip better fits the Granville
vibe—although it's on that section of the street seemingly
reserved for joints that quietly close after a few months of
lacklustre trading. With any luck, this one will make it—if
only for its entertaining gimmick of preparing every dish
on the menu with a dash of alcohol, perfectly reflecting the
Strip's free-drinking ways.

A comfy, windowless combination of dark, clubby bar
and TV-screen-laden sports pub, Sip works hard to be all
things to everyone. You'll find a youngish crowd of pit-
stopping clubbers fuelling up for their next dance-floor
assault as well as backpackers from the nearby hostels
pushing out the boat after a month of living on mystery-
meat pasta. They're lured by live Canucks games and the
DJs that wake up the room around 9:30 PM every night. It's
open to 2 AM, so this is a good late-night haunt.

Take one of the six elevated candlelit tables adjoining
the 50-foot-long suede backrest and kick off with a draft or
two of Stella, Strongbow or the unexpected Éphémère apple
ale from Quebec. A large bottle selection includes Grolsch
and Bud Light Lime, and since this is the party strip, there
are plenty of naughty shooters and cocktails to keep things
moving along: try a traditional absinthe, a Sip Cosmo or the
delightfully named Mind F#*k. Even better is the Diablo,
concocted from vodka, Rose Alize and cranberry.

Keep your liquor intake up with some nosh. Booze
is wedged into every item on the menu here, which
means pricey mains like Bourguignon burgers made with
merlot; maple-glazed sockeye salmon made with sake; and
Portobello cannelloni made with shiraz. Try a couple of
shareable appies instead: the Strongbow mussels, Southern
Comfort spicy chicken and diet-defying lager-battered fries
are good but the vodka-spliced crispy prawn and crab cakes
are the way to go. Just don't blame me if you have a food-
induced hangover in the morning.

Morrissey Irish House

A long, dark meeting-place bar that
ends up keeping you all night

Along with the Lennox at the other end of the Strip, these two pretense-free bars are like bookends for the party-hard nuttiness that routinely characterizes the area. But while the Lennox is bright and functional, the long and narrow Morrissey is dark and seductive—especially in the shabby-chic back area where you could easily sink in for a night of flirty tippling. Trip up the stairs here and grab a pew under the forest of wax-dripped chandeliers that look as though they came straight from a Miss Havisham garage sale.

Alternatively, choose a high side table or a stand-up perch near the bar and check out the talent coming in the front door. With your best *GQ* look, you might even get lucky (or so I'm told), especially on one of the bar's Wednesday-to-Saturday DJ nights. And don't forget to take your time: the Morrissey opens to 2 AM (3 AM Fridays and Saturdays) so your chances will improve in proportion to the amount of alcohol being consumed around you (again, so I'm told).

Alongside a small, half-hearted wine selection and the requisite clutch of naughty cocktails, there's a surprisingly good array of drafts beers here, a holdover from the bar's almost-forgotten Irish pub origins. Quality BC brews like Crannóg Red Branch Ale and Phillips Blue Buck jostle for taste-bud attention with the lip-smacking Blanche de Chambly. The standout is the dark, rare-for-Vancouver Black Widow Ale, a smooth, malty brew from Penticton's Tin Whistle Brewing.

While the weekend party crowd is not usually here to nosh, small plates of spring rolls, crispy calamari or chicken and date skewers are ideal if your group hits a peckish patch. During the week, pub regulars and guests from the adjoining hotel drop in for dinner when the old Irish provenance comes back into play. Along with its chuckwagon deluxe burger, the best grub here includes beef stew and a bulging cottage pie.

Essential tipple Black Widow Ale
Must-have nosh Cottage Pie
Coordinates 1227 Granville Street, 604-682-0909, www.morrisseypub.com

Yale ✪

Vancouver's fancy-free boozy old man . . .
and the Strip's most genuine trad bar

Essential tipple Yale Lager
Must-have nosh BBQ Pork Sandwich
Coordinates 1300 Granville Street, 604-681-9253, www.theyale.ca

The recent history of the Strip is littered with lame-ass bars that came and went faster than a melting ice cube in a hot glass of whisky. But the landmark, brick-built Yale—almost abutting the north side of the Granville Bridge ramp—can trace its provenance right back to the 1800s when it was a bunkhouse for workers in the nearby Yaletown rail yard. In fact, when you step inside the shady interior, there's a strong suspicion that some of those old lags may still be hunkered in the corners knocking back a few cold ones.

While the Yale could easily have gone the way of some of Vancouver's dodgy dive bars, in fact it's become arguably Western Canada's best live blues venue—just check the framed, wall-mounted photos of past performers (yes, that's John Lee Hooker). Ribcage-rattling shows hit the big stage here nightly and while many have cover charges, the majority are free. Attracting a 30-and-over crowd of good-time drinkers and the kind of characters that stay just the right side of legal, sitting anywhere near the front means not having to converse with your drinking buddies.

Alternatively, the sticky tables and grubby carpeted area nearer the entrance feel just like a chatty, old-school boozer, complete with a pair of worn pool tables. Since the clientele here is generally more interested in knocking back quantity rather than comparing lambic tasting notes, the usual blue-collar draft brews are on offer. Additional highlights include Stella, Kilkenny and Guinness and there's even a fancy-free, well-priced Yale Lager that's actually made by Labatt.

The food at the Yale is for refuelling rather than savouring on a gourmet dinner date, which explains the compact selection of standards such as burgers and sandwiches and the appie plates of ribs and chicken fingers. Unusually, an all-day breakfast is also offered, which means you can tuck into your hangover cure before you even leave the bar. The best nosh here, though, is the BBQ Pork Sandwich, prepared with the Yale's house-made Jack Daniels barbecue sauce.

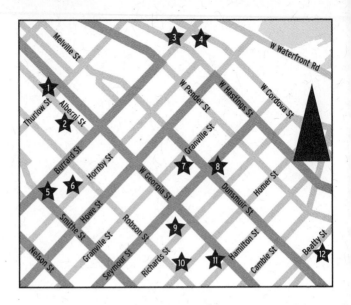

Central Downtown

★1 Shangri-La Market Restaurant Lounge
★2 O Lounge
★3 Elephant & Castle
★4 Lions Pub
★5 Winking Judge Pub
★6 Bacchus Lounge
★7 Shore Club Lounge
★8 Railway Club
★9 Kingston Taphouse
★10 Jimmy's Tap House
★11 Library Square Public House
★12 Chambar

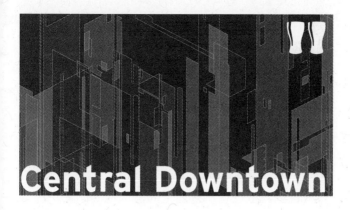

Central Downtown

Sandwiched between Yaletown, Gastown and the West End, the downtown core can be an odd place for a drink. The business district radiating around Burrard and Hastings is a ghost town at night, whereas pockets of activity closer to Robson and Granville lure targeted in-the-know imbibers and wandering, map-wielding tourists with no idea where they are. It's best to have a game plan if you're heading for a drink in this neighbourhood, since aimless bar-hunting can make for a frustrating trawl along dry streets.

Alternatively, cut out the guesswork and make for the Granville Strip, which has so many establishments—not all of them worth hitting—that it's treated to its own chapter here (page 33). With no coordinated scene, there's great diversity to downtown's remaining watering holes, from Brit-style joints like Winking Judge and the Lions to laid-back neighbourhood bars that include Library Square and the Kingston Taphouse. In between, you'll find sophisticated haunts like O Lounge and the slick upstairs bar of the Shangri-La Hotel. For something completely different, though, try downtown's worst-kept bar secret: the second-floor Railway Club is one of Vancouver's best old-school nightlife haunts.

Shangri-La Market Restaurant Lounge

Upscale nook with perfect service
and excellent cocktails

Essential tipple Ginger Margarita

Must-have nosh Rice Cracker Crusted Tuna

Coordinates 1115 Alberni Street, 604-695-1115, www.shangri-la.com

While the lobby bar in Vancouver's tallest hotel tower is fine for a quick drink, it's the luxe third-floor lounge of the high-end Market Restaurant that's your best bet for a night of swanky tippling. The elbow-shaped spot, nestled between the dining room and the patio, includes a long sofa with a string of little candlelit tables. But the best perches are at the shiny black-granite counter opposite. Here you can chat up visiting hotel guests, ogle the urban yuppie crowd and take drink suggestions from the young, friendly and professional bar staff: this is the Shangri-La, so expect personalized service and high standards of drink and dine finesse.

Slide onto your high chair as the sultry lounge music kicks in and peruse the drinks array. In the absence of draft brews, your bottled beers include the likes of Efes, Caracole Troublette, Pyramid Apricot Ale and the smashing Brooklyn Pennant 55. There are also four intriguing ciders—go for Merridale's Cidre Normandie—as well as a comprehensive nine-page wine menu that includes the kind of credit-card-twitching champagnes that are ideal for celebrating a recent billion-dollar stock deal.

Not surprisingly, cocktails are the main lure here and the bar has nailed some highly tempting offerings that should convert the most dedicated of beer drinkers. The refreshing Cucumber Martini is a revelation while the Ginger Margarita is highly addictive. Also check out the five non-alcoholic mixes, including the lip-smacking Cherry Yuzu Soda. Expect a few seasonal additions to both the cocktail and beer selections.

If you're hungry, hit the restaurant (you can also order from its menu in the lounge) or dip into the bar's array of decadent tapas. Dungeness crab cakes and foie gras brûlée are popular but the lovely rice cracker–crusted tuna is recommended. There are also a few tempting larger dishes—mostly gourmet comfort foods—that are surprisingly well priced at under $20 a pop, including a grilled tuna burger and the finger-licking black truffle pizza.

O Lounge

Designer haunt for cocktail tipplers
who've forgotten where Yaletown is

With the sexy aesthetic of a sleek Yaletown bar—not surprisingly, since this is an annex of Coast, a restaurant transplant from that conspicuously bling neighbourhood—O Lounge is one of downtown's hottest places to see and be seen. In fact, if you have the designer duds, laser-whitened teeth and are-they-real-or-not breasts look, you'll fit right in. With my male model good looks, cultivated by years of productive self-delusion, I slid into a corner, assumed my best *GQ* pose and watched the happening scene unfold.

Divided into a decadent front room of mod orange sofas with gold tree-stump side tables and a back room of stand-up light cube perches that look like Star Trek transporter machines (I waited vainly for a cute, green-skinned alien girl to appear), O looks undeniably stylish but also feels intimate. The approach is fuelled by a wait staff composed entirely of attractive young women with winning smiles.

Of course, it's not just about appearances. A small but perfectly formed menu of signature and classic cocktails ranges from a tasty Temptress (gin, cassis, elderflower and strawberries) to a possibly perfect Aviation (gin, maraschino liqueur, lemon and egg white). There's also an impressive two-page wine list focused on New World tipples, including a healthy BC contingent. And if you're gauche enough to need a beer, the bottled Pilsner Urquell is recommended.

Food-wise, aquatic tapas is the main hook—don't forget there's a full restaurant next door if you're starving—and groups should tuck into the magnificent chilled seafood platter, piled high with lobster, crab, prawns and sushi rolls from the raw bar. Once you've had your fill and just before you leave, make sure you peruse your fellow loungers: O is a popular spot for visiting celebs keen to find themselves in local gossip columns. Sadly no one reported my conspicuously showy appearance this time around.

Essential tipple Aviation
Must-have nosh Chilled seafood platter
Coordinates 1054 Alberni Street, 604-685-5010, www.coastrestaurant.ca

Elephant & Castle
A business district favourite that's about
as British as fish and fries

Essential tipple London Pride
Must-have nosh Yorkshire Pudding
Coordinates 385 Burrard Street, 604-696-6730, www.elephantcastle.com

Hitting a Brit-themed bar in North America is an odd experience if you were actually born on the other side of the pond. And Elephant & Castle—tucked into a ground-floor corner of the lovely Art Deco Marine Building—is no exception. Like stepping into a half-remembered dream of an idealized olde worlde tavern (sans features from latter-day Brit pubs like binge-drinking, karaoke nights and noisy slot machines), this visually appealing joint hits all the right fish and chip–loving bases. It's just the kind of place to don your beefeater costume and practise your best UK accent—just remember we call them loos not washrooms.

Joining the local business crowd (they pack the place at lunchtime and haunt the joint after work if they've had a bad day at the office), you'll find a small dark-wood bar, a plethora of stained-glass lamps and those traditional crown-mouldinged high ceilings—along with concessions to North American sensibilities like flatscreen TVs tuned to sports and attractive female wait staff with all their own teeth.

Even the menu is a transatlantic hybrid: heaping shepherd's pie, fish and chips and bangers and mash are here, alongside slightly less traditional "UK dishes" like nachos and calamari. For a true taste of the old country, though, opt for Yorkshire pudding stuffed with beef and served with mash. It's a traditional Brit dish that can only be eaten whilst standing on the table and reciting the national anthem at the top of your voice (just kidding).

Booze-wise, there are some good concessions to the Union Jack here. Yes, there are wines and cocktails that would never be found in some ale-swilling Brit pubs, but there are also some rare-for-Vancouver authentic drafts like Boddingtons, Newcastle Brown and the truly lip-smacking London Pride, a dark and satisfying brew that's usually only found in cans and bottles in Canada. If you choose the Kokanee or Budweiser instead, I will personally hunt you down and sing *Rule Britannia* at you in a slightly unhinged manner.

Lions Pub

Anti-hipster hangout for office
workers and older quaffers

Some bars strive too hard to be like British pubs, but the Lions—the rump at the back of the swanky Terminal City Club—feels like a typical UK boozer without even trying. Scuffed carpets, dinged tables, brass rails and acres of dark-wood panelling line the interior, while the regular crowd of older drinkers, office workers and cruise ship tourists barely straying from their boats make this one of the city's least pretentious watering holes. In fact, this place wouldn't notice a hipster if he strolled in with a neon-pink zebra for company (call ahead before you try this).

A labyrinth of little tables, especially in the shady corners at the back, this is the kind of bar that invites its patrons to chat over a few bevies rather than rely for entertainment on noisy piped-in music or sports-spewing TV screens (there are only a couple here and most tables don't face them). There's also a viewless, concrete-lined patio out front that's only worth considering if you haven't been outside for a year or two.

Once you've found your perch, you'll be faced with an impressive array of on-tap brews including Smithwicks, Boddingtons, the full Granville Island roster and a pair of Vancouver Island favourites from Lighthouse Brewing Company (Beacon IPA is recommended). There's even a pair of choice Belgian taps, including the popular Hoegaarden white beer and the excellent Leffe Blonde Abbey Ale, strong enough to put hairs on the chests of everyone sitting around you.

The usual hearty pub grub suspects are on offer, along with a couple of choice faves like salmon burgers and butter chicken curry (another echo of contemporary British pubs), but the Ploughman's Lunch is recommended. The UK's main concession to the concept of salad, this one authentically favours bread, two cheeses and cold cuts over its veggies—although unlike in England, the greenery here is not just for decoration.

Essential tipple Beacon IPA
Must-have nosh Ploughman's Lunch
Coordinates 888 West Cordova Street, 604-488-8602, www.tcclub.com

Winking Judge Pub

Compact, Brit-style snug with hearty
nosh and an eclectic crowd

Essential tipple Strongbow **Must-have nosh** Bangers and Mash **Coordinates** 888 Burrard Street, 604-684-9465, www.winkingjudgepub.com

Adding to downtown's surfeit of expat pubs, this new UK kid on the block is a chatty, Brit-ish bar possibly designed by someone who hasn't set foot in the real thing since 1978. The Winking Judge—named for its proximity to the BC Supreme Court—is an odd, L-shaped little nook that lures a strange mix of patrons. Slide into a corner and you'll overhear T-shirted twentysomethings discussing the latest *Transformers* flick at the nearby multiplex, then you'll catch an earful from middle-aged gripers in town from the suburbs for their monthly steak-and-ale pie fix. And if it's a balmy summer night, the little patio out front will be packed, despite the fact that it hugs the noisy Burrard and Smithe intersection.

Decor-wise, the interior here is just as eclectic as the clientele. While floor-to-ceiling windows line two sides of the room, the rest is studded with retro booze adverts, prints of kilted soldiers and a moth-eaten stag's head that looks more than ready for a stiff drink. It's the kind of oddball collection of junkshop stuff that could have been scooped up from a garage sale on a wet Sunday in London.

Lacking any on-tap UK beers—Guinness doesn't count—you can sip bottles of Bass, Boddingtons and Newcastle Brown here. Alternatively, indulge in a draft pint of Strongbow cider or several ubiquitous Canadian brews. Arguably, the food is a bigger lure. Although the punning menu goes overboard with groan-worthy meal monikers like Big Ben Burgers, Princess Margaret Pizzas and Westminster Mis-Steaks, the entrees have a hearty, home-cooked feel that make them worth saving your hunger for. In fact, the four-banger sausage and mash, with a mound of fluffy potato swimming in a sea of thick gravy, should easily keep you going for the rest of the week.

Bacchus Lounge
Decadent bar with a sumptuous, gentleman's club élan

It's a shame smoking is banned in Vancouver, since there isn't a better place in the city where the idea of slowly puffing on a giant Cuban (the stogie, not the person) seems so right. You'll just have to content yourself with donning a velvet jacket, sinking into a crushed-satin chair and warming your blue-chip shares at the large open fireplace. Welcome to Bacchus in the Wedgewood Hotel, where wealthy traditionalists like to hang out before dinner or just chill after a hard day on the golf course in shaded, dark-wood splendour.

Of course the tourists slightly lower the tone. One minute you're ordering from a starched, waist-coated server, the next a hotel guest strolls in wearing jeans and a polo shirt as if he owns the place. Puff an imaginary smoke ring in his direction and bury your face in the drinks list and he might just go away.

You'll find a cursory gesture to beer here, but anyone offering Coors and Kokanee clearly holds this particular beverage in contempt (the draft Guinness is your best bet). Instead, take refuge in a cocktail list that hits all the bases. The decadent Hennessy Olympic City (Vancouver) includes Triple Sec, lemon juice and a twist of lemon peel—perhaps ironically, it's also one of the priciest drinks on offer. Instead, try the recommended Red Satin Slip, an addictive Bacchus fave concocted from Smirnoff, raspberry liqueur, cranberry juice and fresh lime.

Along with the excellent wine list (try the Oyster Bay Sauvignon Blanc) and a gold-standard whisky array of major hits and lesser-known treats—including a 16-year-old Lagavulin—the food offerings are surprisingly well priced. Mains like sirloin burgers and thin-crust pizzas (go for the salmon) are under $20, but the swanky room seems to better suit more restrained tasting plates like truffle oil–drizzled fries. In fact, your best option—especially with an accompanying glass of Taylor Fladgate by the fire—is a plate of savour-worthy Canadian cheeses. Just make sure you include the smashing Little Qualicum Cheeseworks brie in your selection.

Essential tipple Red Satin Slip
Must-have nosh Cheese Plate
Coordinates 845 Hornby Street, 604-608-5319, www.wedgewoodhotel.com

Shore Club Lounge

Slick business meeting hangout
for passing millionaires

If transacting multi-million-dollar business deals over decadent drinks is part of your world, you've probably already been to the sleekly cavernous Shore Club. If not, you may have tried unsuccessfully to peer through the wooden blinds at the corner of Granville and Dunsmuir on your way to the nearby Tim Hortons. But even if your budget resides firmly at street-urchin level, it's worth pushing though the frosted-glass doors (smart casual dress required) to see how the other half lives.

Part of the Hy group that includes the similarly exclusive Gotham Steakhouse, the sumptuous bi-level interior here is lined (including the ceiling) with cherry wood panelling studded with Art Deco flourishes, including angular light shades and inlaid elevator doors. It's like boarding a contemporary recreation of a 1930s ocean liner—on the first-class deck of course.

While dinner is served upstairs to the captains of industry, the granite-countered ground-level lounge bar is perfect for some fat-cat hobnobbing. You can fit in by checking your stocks on the wall-mounted TV screens or tapping your toes to the piano player tinkling the ivories in the corner on most nights.

The lounge's impressively thick wine list offers full pages of French, Italian, Australian and BC tipples (Mission Hill Oculus included) plus 19 champagnes ranging up to an eye-watering $490 per bottle—ideal for celebrating that just-completed takeover. Cocktails slake most thirsts here, though: try the Afternoon Delight, expertly concocted from Grey Goose Vodka (of course), Malibu Mango Rum and guava and pineapple juices.

Once you've downed a few, alongside some seafood-focused tapas including a recommended three-part tartare (snapper, salmon and tuna), consider ending the evening with an 18-year-old Macallan single-malt nightcap. Then hit the cold, mean streets with the few remaining coins jangling in your pocket. Those Timbits are just a short stroll away.

Essential tipple Afternoon Delight
Must-have nosh Trio of Fish Tartare
Coordinates 688 Dunsmuir Street, 604-899-4400, www.theshoreclub.ca

Railway Club

Warm, old-school city centre bar with choice
microbrews, eclectic decor and diverse live music

It's late Friday night at a rickety corner table in a cozy upstairs
watering hole that's ringing with animated chat. Surveying
the scene, you watch a pair of laughing student girls swiftly
sipping ciders behind two oblivious old duffers who look
like they've been propping up the bar all day. The room's
dinged chairs are all full, dimpled pint glasses are being
drained at a merry rate and even the model train trundling
around the ceiling past UK bus signs and dog-eared band
posters looks like it's having a good time. Welcome to the
Rail, Vancouver's most beloved trad drinking spot.

Built more than 70 years ago as a working men's club for
railway employees, generations of curious Vancouverites have
pushed through the heavy wooden door near the 7-Eleven,
climbed the scuffed carpeted stairway and "discovered" a
laid-back joint that welcomes everyone from office workers
to tie-dyed bohemians. They come to chat with buddies
they know will be here, sup well-priced microbrews from
proper beer glasses and check out a nightly changing roster
of live music that's even more eclectic than the regulars—
think beat poets, singer-songwriters and accordion rappers.
There's usually no cover charge before 8 PM but consider
paying anyway to support the performers.

Stepping up to the bar (unusually, there's no table service
here), make sure you peruse the specials board before hitting
the crowded clutch of ever-changing taps, often including
treats from Crannóg, Phillips, Tree Brewing and beyond. Big
Rock is also a mainstay and there's usually at least one lip-
smacking offering from Surrey's surprisingly good Central
City Brewing. If it's the end of the night and you need a
pick-me-up to make it home, try an Espresso Martini. And
if you're hungry, the Rail's late-night hole-in-the-wall hatch
can sort you out with hearty plates of nachos, pizzas or even
a Cobb salad—a far better idea than the cheap pizza joints
that will be luring to you outside.

Essential tipple Central City Big Kettle ESB
Must-have nosh Chicken Quesadillas
Coordinates 579 Dunsmuir Street, 604-681-1625, www.therailwayclub.com

Kingston Taphouse

Laid-back favourite with a hidden double
patio beloved of in-the-know regulars

Essential tipple Hop Head IPA

Must-have nosh Flat Iron Steak Sandwich

Coordinates 755 Richards Street, 604-681-7011, www.kingstontaphouse.com

For all you beer-stained old Vancouver barflies out there (you know who you are), let's share a moment of silence—which means no burping—for the fondly remembered Rose and Thorn, which pulled its last pint of grog in this location a few years ago. Now let's forget about it and move on to the great neighbourhood bar that replaced it. And stop blubbing; you're wasting valuable drinking time.

It's easy to walk past the darkened storefront of the Kingston without even noticing it. But once you're inside, you'll be blown away by how large it is—we're talking two interior floors plus a double-decker patio hidden out back. The comfy interior is fine on chilly nights, with its classic sports bar look of hardwood floors, sought-after booths and a surfeit of small tables with leather-look chairs.

But if it's a balmy summer evening, the twin alfresco areas are the main lure. The larger second-floor patio is tucked at the back of the building and is ideal for an intimate chat, but weave up the stairs to the top level and you'll have a starry night-sky canopy to quaff under. Popular with in-the-know-locals (which now includes you), it's one of the city's best outdoor drinking spots.

Among the Kingston's draft brews, you'll find BC faves like Red Truck Ale and Tree Brewing's lip-smacking Hop Head. There are also three signature "Kingston beers" that are actually concocted by Granville Island Brewing. Wine lovers are well served, too, with selections from Inniskillin, Burrowing Owl and beyond. Whatever your choose, round it off with a Kingston Martini, made with vodka, mandarin orange and passion-fruit liqueur. They slip down rather easily, so don't start the evening with them or you'll be falling off the patio before midnight.

Grub-wise, the Kingston offers tweaked bar classics—check the changing weekly specials board—including the recommended tuna Caesar salad, kung pao chicken and a flat iron steak sandwich that has an understandably enthusiastic following. And for lighter fare, the firecracker shrimp serves as an ideal tapas plate.

Jimmy's Tap House

Friendly downtown sports bar with a winning patio

With those looming glass towers hogging all the views, downtown bars are almost totally lacking in patios. Those that do exist are usually unloved adjuncts tacked on at street level and barely divided from our persistent sidewalk panhandlers by rickety railings. One of the rare exceptions is Jimmy's, an otherwise unassuming sports bar with a raised alfresco deck that's almost bigger than its interior. It's the main reason for coming here, unless you need to hunker down inside for the latest live UFC scrap (for the biggest bouts, they'll drag a flatscreen onto the patio).

Despite it being a self-described tap house, Jimmy's regulars—construction workers from all those half-built towers hanging out after a hard day's graft—are often happiest chugging pitchers of ice-cold Canadian and Budweiser. But for tipple connoisseurs (think slower-drinking office workers and Yaletownites straying up the street from their usual haunts), there's a happening array of drafts like Kilkenny, Stella Artois and a couple of Russell Brewing offerings—their Lemon Ale is especially popular in summer. Aiming to please everyone, cocktails, whiskies and a few wine offerings round out the beverage mix.

The food selection—check the specials before you order—is similarly diverse, moving beyond sports bar classics like burgers and chicken strips to slightly more upmarket fare that would be at home on an Earl's menu (jambalaya and Cajun halibut salad spring to mind). But the best Jimmy's nosh is the hearty grub built to fill a construction worker's boots. The bulging lasagna, stuffed with meat, edam and mozzarella and served with garlic toast is the appetite equivalent of wrestling a bear and is ideal if you haven't eaten in a week. And if you've had a few too many brews here the night before, it's worth coming back for a groggy-eyed weekend brunch, sensibly served until 3 PM.

Essential tipple Russell Cream Ale
Must-have nosh Lasagna
Coordinates 783 Homer Street, 604-689-2800, www.jimmystaphouse.com

Library Square Public House

Large, dark, cave-like pub that hits all the
right neighbourhood bar buttons

Essential tipple Big Rock Traditional Ale

Must-have nosh Bacon Cheddar Burger

Coordinates 300 West Georgia Street, 604-633-9644, www.donnellypubs.ca

Although attached limpet-like to downtown's Coliseum-esque library, this laid-back neighbourhood bar is just about the last place you'd overhear a conversation on Proust or Camus. But what Library Square lacks in intellectual pretense, it more than makes up for in its comfy, no-nonsense approach to liquid-fuelled leisure.

The kind of place you'd drop into for a solitary lunchtime pint, then return with friends for a lively evening of DJ tunes, music quizzes or broadcast sports (check the website and pick your preferred night), soccer fans should take particular note: live Glasgow Celtic and England games—presumably not on the same night—lure packs of scarf-clad nuts no matter what time of day they occur. Anyone for a 7 AM kickoff and a pint of grog?

Not that you'd ever know what time of day it is here anyway. Almost every surface in this cavernous, near-windowless bar is painted black and you'll feel like you're cocooned inside on a rainy day even when the sun is shining—unless you hit the drafty afterthought of a patio huddling in near-permanent shadow outside. Stay indoors (preferably at one of the cable spool tables that resemble giant upturned cotton reels) and you'll get the full pub effect.

Drinks-wise, the Granville Island Brewing roster is on permanent special. But if you're feeling a little more adventurous, consider a Crown Float (Guinness and cider), a Black and Tan (Guinness and pale ale) or the excellent Big Rock Trad Ale, Alberta's second-most lucrative liquid export. For a chaser, there's also a surprisingly good whisky selection, including the pricey Johnnie Walker Blue Label.

Soak up the booze with typical pub grub classics like steaks, BLTs and fish and chips, but make sure you check the specials board: a good-value beer and burger deal will likely be winking right back at you.

Chambar

Romantic candlelit cocoon that's perfect
for a flirty affair with Belgian brews

Essential tipple Chambar Ale
Must-have nosh Congolaise Moules Frites
Coordinates 562 Beatty Street, 604-879-7119, www.chambar.com

If you hunker down on one of the sought-after comfy sofas
by the door or just perch at the glossy L-shaped bar, it's easy
to forget that brick-lined Chambar is also one of Vancouver's
most celebrated restaurants. But if you're a gourmet booze
hound, this is simply an excellent spot to indulge your
naughty predilection for seductive Belgian beer—treated
here with the kind of sophistication, food-pairing respect
and all-round savour-worthy reverence usually reserved
for fine wines. In fact, this place is like a wine bar for beer
lovers.

Not to suggest that they don't serve wine here. In fact,
there's an impressive four-page selection (splash out on a
Felton Road Riesling if you're feeling flush) plus a 10-tipple
array of well-executed cocktails (the famed Blue Fig Martini
is the way to go). But the smartly dressed crowd of rich
professionals and coiffured Yaletown expats dressed for a
night of sultry shenanigans is just as likely to be indulging
in the revelatory roster of lambics, tripels and Trappistes.

There's a revolving roster of five drafts, plus a huge list
of exotic bottles. The friendly wait staff will happily suggest
something to suit your palate but virgins should start with
the marvelously rich signature Chambar Ale draft before
diving into unfamiliar but rewarding bottles like the eye-
popping champagne-style Brut des Flanders. And don't
forget that handy Czech proverb while you're at it: "A fine
beer may be judged with only one sip . . . but it's better to
be thoroughly sure."

Befitting its quality-restaurant provenance, hungry
quaffers can hit recommended mains like roasted halibut or
braised lamb shank. But if you're more intent on weaving
your way down the beer list and just need a sustenance pit
stop, go for the Moules Frites. Served in three mouthwatering
varieties, the spicy Congolaise version is best. It comes in
tomato-coconut cream with smoked chili and lime. Possibly
not the side dish that Belgian monks enjoyed when they
were perfecting their beer recipes in the medieval era.

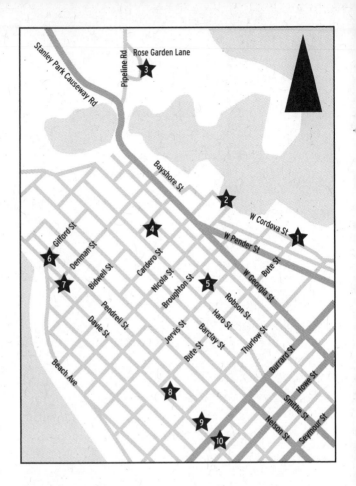

West End

⭐ Mill Marine Bistro
⭐ Cardero's (Live Bait Marine Pub)
⭐ Stanley's Park Bar & Grill
⭐ Guu with Garlic
⭐ O'Doul's
⭐ Sylvia's Lounge
⭐ Bayside Lounge
⭐ 1181
⭐ Fountainhead Pub
⭐ Bin 941

West End

Everyone knows two things about the West End: it's one of North America's most densely populated neighbourhoods and it's home to Canada's largest gay community. Both facts inform the area's lively drinking scene. Bustling bars stud the main Robson and Denman thoroughfares, while Coal Harbour has a couple of winning waterfront spots that are popular with locals and tourists alike. Heading to Davie Street, you'll find a kaleidoscope of gay-friendly bars alongside the pink-painted bus shelters and rainbow-striped flags.

Whatever your inclination, variety is the spice of drinking life here. The snug drinkery at Cardero's is highly welcoming; intimate Bin 941 is possibly the city's best late-night tapas bar; and the Mill offers probably Vancouver's best nature-hugging vistas from its panoramic patio. In-the-know sunset-viewing fans are also well served at English Bay's retro Bayside Lounge as well as at the comfy, old-school bar of the nearby Sylvia Hotel. And if you fancy a side order of free live jazz, a perch at O'Douls is worth dropping in for. Of course, if your idea of a good night out includes a little same-sex flirting, 1181 or the Fountainhead Pub may well be the way to go.

Mill Marine Bistro

An outdoor-hugging bar where you'll
soon be drunk on the scenery

Essential tipple Brain Freeze Slushy Must-have nosh Whistler Beer Mussels Coordinates 1199 West Cordova Street, 604-687-6455, www.millbistro.ca

It's 3 PM on one of those languid summertime afternoons in blue-skied Vancouver and you've managed to sneak away from your desk without anyone noticing. Rather than spend the time hiding from co-workers in a shopping mall, wind your way to the waterfront Mill and you'll find you're not the only one who's abandoned his post. Duck under a red parasol, slide into a rickety plastic table and drink deeply of the kind of view that makes starry-eyed tourists click their way impulsively to the Immigration Canada website.

With its spectacular panorama of gently lapping shoreline, Stanley Park's forested fringes and the looming dark crags of the North Shore mountains, the Mill doesn't have to try too hard to lure its customers—if it was located anywhere else, it would be just another humdrum neighbourhood drinkery. But with Vancouver's best patio views, it's the number one place to be on a sunny afternoon. There's a gesture towards inside seating of course (this is the Wet Coast after all), but the sprawling outdoor patio is what it's all about—in fact, even the washrooms are in a building next door that doubles as a public facility.

If you're not already drunk on the scenery, there's a full complement of Whistler Brewing beers (the copper-coloured Pale Ale is best) plus the usual Granville Island Brewing drafts. All are served in sleeve size or, for a dollar more, the 20oz "Mill size" that's otherwise known as a pint. There are also a few choice wines, such as Okanagan faves from Sandhill and Mission Hill, along with a list of Caesars including oddball varieties with quail's eggs and wild salmon. Instead, have a summer-friendly Brain Freeze Slushy of mango, vodka and lemonade while the evening sun slowly slinks away. And if you haven't covered all the food groups with your Bacon N' Egger Caesar, dive into a brothy bowl of beer mussels.

Cardero's (Live Bait Marine Pub)

Snug, sea-salt-flavoured side bar
with good aquatic nosh

Hands up if you know where the Live Bait Marine Pub is. Thought not. How about Cardero's? Yes, me too. If you've ever heard anyone using the ridiculous official name of the little bar that clings like a barnacle to its Coal Harbour restaurant sibling, I might buy you a drink (you'll have to catch me first). But there's no need to get hung up on monikers here. Just tell everyone to meet you at "Cardero's Pub" and then arrive early enough to snag the best seat: in winter, it's a saggy leather sofa huddled near the roaring corner stove.

Perched on piles alongside a flotilla of shiny pleasure vessels, this cozy, deck-floored snug is often missed by hungry noshers flocking to the restaurant's expansive patio. But the pub shares the same menu and its picture windows offer similar boat-bobbing views. Lined with model ships, steam-liner prints and assorted maritime paraphernalia, it's also the perfect place to hunker down in the shadows pretending to be the old sea dog character from *Jaws*. Make sure you have plenty of good scars to show off.

While die-hard sea salts will probably drink anything, you can afford to be more discerning here. The dozen drafts include Strongbow, Guinness, Red Truck Lager and the recommended Okanagan Spring Pale Ale. For something a little more exotic, there's a good Seabreeze Martini (Smirnoff, lemon juice and sugar rum), while a glass or two of smooth Bushmills can pickle the gills of any passing sailor. There's also live music of the guitar-and-cover-songs variety every night expect Fridays and Saturdays, when the bar is too crowded for entertainers.

If lining your stomach before heading out on the high seas is a priority—ship's biscuits are a poor substitute for a good meal—Cardero's offers high-end aquatic entrees more suited to the adjoining restaurant. But it's the pub grub that's more at home on this side of the pond: hearty clam chowder, followed by a bulging burger crammed with deep-fried oysters will set you up for any upcoming voyage.

Essential tipple Okanagan Spring Pale Ale
Must-have nosh Oyster Burger
Coordinates 1583 Coal Harbour Quay, 604-669-7666, www.vancouverdine.com

Stanley's Park Bar & Grill
Tree-hugging tipple perch in the heart of the park

Essential tipple Life's a Peach

Must-have nosh Hummus and Pita

Coordinates 610 Pipeline Road, 604-602-3088, www.stanleysbar.ca

A 10-minute walk into Stanley Park from the West Georgia Street entrance and tucked into one side of the century-old Pavilion building—an evocative reminder of the old-school leisure facilities that dotted the park in its early years—it's hard to beat the nature-hugging location of this tourist-luring drink and dine spot. Nestled among towering Douglas fir trees and only open June to September, you'll find yourself rubbing shoulders with guidebook-clutching international visitors who are fuelling up before strolling to their next totem-pole photo shoot.

While the bar's small interior is little more than a glossy-countered shelter from summertime rain storms, the expansive patio—more than three times bigger than the inside area—is what it's all about. Duck under a red parasol here and slide alongside a plastic table for some tranquil quaffing, then consider sticking around to check out an energetic Theatre Under the Stars show at the Malkin Bowl just a few feet away. Alternatively, you can hear all the songs from your patio perch if you just want a free live soundtrack to accompany your drink.

There's a limited selection of food and drinks here, presumably aimed at tourists who don't know any better. Avoid the main dishes—mostly overpriced burger and fish and chips offerings—and instead share a plate of hummus and pita with a few choice bevies. Part of the local mini-chain that also owns the Mill, the full Whistler Brewing beer retinue is available here, plus a pair of Granville Island brews and some bottled Sol, Guinness and Stella Artois options. Instead, consider the Life's a Peach alcoholic slushy, made with vodka and peach liqueur. On a balmy summer evening, it slides down faster than a squirrel on a greased tree trunk.

Guu with Garlic

Immersive izakaya with young vibe, friendly
staff and great deep-fried nosh

If you've taught ESL in Tokyo you'll be familiar with the
inside of a few grungy izakayas, Japan's down-home version
of the neighbourhood bar. Having spent many nights
staggering from the warmth of a clamorous, paper-walled
barroom after a session of Sapporo and greasy snacks, I've
been ever-hungry for the same experience this side of the
pond. Luckily, Vancouver izakayas have sprung up like wild
mushrooms after a monsoon.

While most are slick restaurant versions of the concept,
the Guu mini-chain—especially their Robson and Bidwell
location—hits the spot. Arrive around the 5:30 PM opening
time for a seat at the L-shaped wooden bar. You'll be
greeted by welcoming shouts from the young staff (at least
I think that's what they were saying) and handed a sheaf of
menus. All is in English but the staffers are happy to offer
recommendations—take them up on this.

From your bar perch, you can watch the kitchen whirling
through its orders as a funky '70s movie soundtrack keeps
things lively. Your fellow noshers will be mostly Asian
students at the chunky wooden tables or on the little side
patio visible through the lattice windows. By mid-evening,
you'll feel fully immersed in another culture.

Drinks-wise, Kirin and Asahi drafts dominate, but make
sure you also include a hot or cold sake or an intriguing
Japanese-style cocktail. If you're a true recovering ESL
teacher, you'll also need some nostalgic shochu, the rocket
fuel distilled rice vodka that was cheaper and stronger than
sake when I was out there.

Soak up the booze with some deep-fried Japanese
comfort food. Steaming noodle dishes and oden hotpots are
offered, but the well-priced tapas plates are recommended.
Go for creamy potato croquettes, boiled eggs in deep-fried
pumpkin balls and the recommended tori-karaage chicken.
The Japanese equivalent of chicken strips, it's a hearty
serving for two and comes in a bamboo basket. Keep in
mind that this Guu outlet is garlic-obsessed, so you'll find it
added liberally to most dishes.

Essential tipple Shochu
Must-have nosh Tori-karaage Chicken
Coordinates 1698 Robson Street, 604-685-8678, www.guu-izakaya.com

O'Douls

Dark little jazz hangout with an
impressive draft selection

Essential tipple Storm Black Plague Stout
Must-have nosh Ocean Trio
Coordinates 1300 Robson Street, 604-661-1400, www.odoulsrestaurant.com

Favoured by visiting Jazz Fest musicians who drop in after
their main shows to jam the night away, the permanently
mood-lit little bar at O'Doul's is ideal for a cozy night out.
And you don't even have to wait for the festival to catch
some easy-listening vibes: there's smooth, cover-free jazz
music here every night with piano tinklers the first half of
the week and toe-tapping trios the second half. Of course
they're mainly playing to the adjoining restaurant, but
quaffers balancing on high chairs at the bar or embedded in
the soft-backed seats lining the walls can also enjoy them.

Expect chatty service from the barman here and make
sure you ask him for a few drink suggestions. While the
bar menu lists only a few wines, you can also tap into the
impressive 350-bottle selection on offer to restaurant patrons
(the Okanagan's Blue Mountain Pinot Noir is worth a sip
or two). Additionally, there's an impressive array of house
cocktails (Gimlets, Seabreezes and Brown Cows included),
plus some whisky-based martinis and an extensive selection
of liqueur nightcaps.

For such a small bar, there's a truly amazing array
of carefully chosen draft beers, with not a single dud in
sight. BC craft brews are a specialty, with Hermann's
Dark Bavarian Lager, Crannóg's Red Branch Irish Ale,
the relatively new Stanley Park 1897 Amber from Turning
Point Brewery, and the richly satisfying Black Plague Stout
from Commercial Drive's celebrated Storm Brewing. Don't
worry if the choice seems overwhelming, it's hard to choose
anything you won't enjoy.

Food-wise, there's a focus on grease-free tapas, with the
Ocean Trio plate of regional salmon, mussels and shrimp
cakes standing out. There's also some added sustenance
next door: stroll along the corridor towards the Listel Hotel
lobby and you'll find a hidden little art gallery room with a
focus on contemporary works.

Sylvia's Lounge

Comfy as an old armchair with killer beachfront views

Opened in the mid-1950s, the wood-lined character lounge at the ivy-sheathed Sylvia Hotel was originally Vancouver's first cocktail bar. While its VIP-luring days are long gone, it's since become a smashing neighbourhood haunt for savvy West Enders who like chatting in cozy comfort while stealing sidelong glances at English Bay's sunset panoramas. It's hard to imagine a more relaxing spot for an evening beverage among friends—just make sure you arrive before them so you can snag one of the view-tastic window seats.

There's a retro feel to the bar here, triggered by warmly glowing wall lamps and the kind of well-maintained beechwood tables and vinyl easy chairs now only found in the mothballed basement suites of your grandparents' house. It's a comfy, pretense-free approach that means everyone, from hipsters to ancients, feels instantly welcome and often stays a little longer than originally planned.

There are four well-priced local brews on offer—two each from Russell Brewing and Granville Island (the new Brockton IPA is worth a swig)—plus bottles of Red Stripe and Alexander Keith's. But why not recall the glory days with some signature cocktails? The 1954 (vodka, Chambord liqueur, lime and muddled raspberries and blueberries) is justifiably popular, as is the excellent Sylvia Caesar, complete with a pickled bean and a prawn garnish. But if you're facing a cold, windswept beachfront in the dead of winter, consider a warming blueberry tea with Grand Marnier and Amaretto.

For the rabidly esurient, there's an adjoining restaurant (you can order anything from its menu in the bar, too) as well as a good selection of bar-specific nosh. The excellent nachos are well worth a dip, while curried shrimp sandwich and Thai shrimp salad are also popular. But it's the stuffed mushrooms—crammed with crab, shrimp, roasted garlic and two types of cheese—that are a Sylvia must-have. It's the kind of dish that'll take you right back to the good old days.

Essential tipple Sylvia Caesar
Must-have nosh Stuffed Mushrooms
Coordinates 1154 Gilford Street, 604-681-9321, www.sylviahotel.com

Bayside Lounge

Retro-look upstairs joint with spectacular
sunset views over English Bay

Essential tipple Bayside Delight
Must-have nosh Seafood Clubhouse
Coordinates 1755 Davie Street, 604-682-1831, www.bestwesternsandshotelvancouver.com

Another local favourite with loyal in-the-know followers, trudging upstairs to the well-hidden Bayside Lounge is like stepping back into 1978, when brown and burgundy vinyl ruled the world. But retro aesthetics are not the main visual lure here. Like a UFO perched atop the corner of Davie and Denman, you'll find a circular room with a low-slung, perfectly round bar plus a large, curving window offering panoramic views over palm-fringed English Bay. Snagging one of the little tables facing this waterfront eye candy is one of the best ways to enjoy a Vancouver sunset.

If you can tear yourself away from the views, the Bayside chefs-up a good selection of martinis and cocktails (the Bayside Delight—vodka, melon, lime, mint and cranberry—is a refreshing favourite) plus a fairly standard beer list that's enlivened by the presence of the recommended darkly pleasing R & B Red Devil Pale Ale. Check the daily specials: there's always something cheap and cheerful to wet your whistle.

Grub-wise, bar-style comfort food is the approach, although dishes like the seafood clubhouse and Teriyaki pineapple burger elevate things to just above the ordinary. If you're simply craving some salty finger food with your drinks, the nachos and yam fries are justifiably popular, while there's a regular wing special every day from 3 PM to 7 PM.

The Bayside is also a rare West End late-night haunt. You can slide in here until 2 AM (3 AM on Fridays and Saturdays) when you'll be serenaded nightly by DJs spinning old and new sounds to keep you awake. The late crowd is surprisingly diverse, including plenty of staff from area bars and restaurants dropping by to bitch about their customers plus a few red-nosed barflies that probably don't even know what time of day it is.

1181

The West End's coolest gay bar

In a gaybourhood full of pub-style pick-up joints, this sleek but laid-back lounge is a welcome alternative. As long and narrow as Noel Coward's cigarette holder, the candlelit room here has a slick West Coast look comprising a chatty sofa-strewn area at the front and a cozy back haunt where couples like to hang out—often to watch the movies playing on the wall (vintage *Logan's Run* on my visit).

Dividing the two areas is a slender bar staffed by friendly, T-shirt-clad servers. Perching singletons sit at the counter here and watch the room like hawks, waiting for fresh talent to arrive. While 1181 is not as raucous as some of the scene's other bars, it's just as active on the flirtation front, although the regulars generally don't feel the need to sport lederhosen to advertise their availability. Frequently described as Vancouver's most straight-friendly gay bar, DJs stoke up a clubby atmosphere here on Wednesday to Saturday nights. And then there's Sunday afternoons, when the bar opens early to let the local drag queens strut their stuff.

The fuel for all this fun is clearly the giant drinks selection, presented in a thick leather folder. The bottled beer offerings are fairly standard, while the wine is mostly New World—including quaffable BC treats from Inniskillin, Gray Monk and Cedar Creek. But it's the cocktail list that stands out better than a pink-painted bus shelter in a town full of Texas rednecks.

There's a page of classics (including a good Manhattan) followed by an eclectic contemporary selection divided into fresh, fruity, savoury, floral and tart pages. The signature 1181 Margarita (with Cointreau and lime-infused tequila) is justly popular, while the fruity Blueboy (Berry Skyy vodka, raspberry and youngberry) lures many to a night of ruin. And it's hard to imagine the Knock Out (Tanqueray, passion fruit and lime) having a better name. Hopefully these libations will satisfy you since this is one of the only bars in Vancouver that doesn't serve food.

Essential tipple 1181 Margarita
Must-have nosh Another 1181 Margarita
Coordinates 1181 Davie Street, 604-687-3991, www.tightlounge.com

Fountainhead Pub

Neighbourhood hangout for the
Davie Street party crowd

Essential tipple Dead Frog Nut Brown Ale

Must-have nosh Regular J Burger

Coordinates 1025 Davie Street, 604-687-2222, www.thefountainheadpub.com

You don't have to be gay to drink here but it probably helps, especially if your idea of a good time is wolf-whistling preening locals from the party-like patio in the heart of Vancouver's Davie Street gaybourhood. Alongside a streetscape of rainbow flag decals, you can same-sex flirt to your heart's content at the Fountainhead. And if you're straight, you can grab a brew, munch on pub grub classics and watch the patio shenanigans with an amusedly raised eyebrow.

The interior's dinged dark-wood furnishings, grubby old carpets and popular pool table echo neighbourhood bars just about anywhere. But the thumping disco soundtrack and paintings of full-frontal naked fellas lining one wall give the game away slightly—it's the kind of artwork generally absent from your average Fogg 'N' Suds. And if you want to hit that patio, arrive early (especially on weekends) or you'll have to sulk inside and add your name to the designated chalkboard in the hope that a space will open up.

Check the daily specials board above the window before ordering your poison: there's usually a $4 beer or (less often) a $5 wine available. While there's a fairly extensive and well-priced draft beer selection—including Dead Frog Nut Brown Ale and Alexander Keith's Red Amber Ale—there are also some naughtily named shots and cocktails, including Porn Star, Slippery Nipple, Sicilian Kiss and several others with names slightly too risqué to mention here.

Food-wise, you'll find all the usual pub grub suspects, plus a few tweaked specials like the wasabi salmon burger, sweet chicken curry salad and the popular Montreal smoked-meat sandwich. You can't go wrong with the Regular J Burger, though. Packed with mushrooms, bacon and cheese, it's the ideal fuel for a sweaty night of Davie Street clubbing.

Bin 941

Hopping little late-night party room
with a winning vibe and great tapas

Pioneering the contemporary tapas bar concept long before it became a Vancouver trend, tiny Bin 941 still hits the spot. Smaller and correspondingly vibier than its West Broadway sibling (Bin 942), arrive as soon after the 5 PM opening as possible to ensure one of the sought-after tables—the two comfy, people-watching window nooks are best but a perch at the bar can be just as much fun. Once the clubby music starts pumping and the art-lined room takes on a golden, candlelit glow, you'll feel like you're in a private party with a bunch of new-found friends.

The room is swinging by 10 PM, when animated conversations spill invitingly onto Davie Street, but a snug, mellow vibe takes hold later as the bar winds down to its 2 AM closing. By this stage, with the booze taking hold, you'll sit back and start noticing the artwork—including that arched-back black cat on the wall opposite the counter.

While the music is sometimes too loud to chat here (942 is a bit quieter), your mouth will be otherwise engaged on a dedicated course of imbibing. Around two-dozen wines, each available by the glass, are on offer with both the Old and New Worlds represented, including a few BC treats (look out for Joie Rosé). If you prefer a beer, consider the drafts from R&B and Red Truck, including some seasonal specials. Tempting liquors and cocktails (designated Lustful, Flirtatious and Horny Stuff on the menu) cry out for some late-night sipping, including the Bingria, a house sangria featuring apricot brandy.

And even if you're not hungry, it's impossible not to be tempted by the innovative small-plates menu. The "Tapatisers" include great sharing plates like tuna tartare, black cod, beef tenderloin Wellington and the unmissable crab cakes, served with burnt-orange chipotle sauce. But if you're still here by 1:30 AM, when the kitchen closes, grab some finger-licking satay sticks to keep you going until your make it home (the lamb Tandoori is recommended).

Essential tipple Bingria
Must-have nosh Crab Cakes
Coordinates 941 Davie Street, 604-683-1246, www.bin941.com

On the road in the Lower Mainland

It's easy to dismiss the burbs for offering nothing more than a wasteland of crummy sports bars and rough-and-ready redneck boozers, where drinking to oblivion is the preferred strategy. But not every bar in Surrey, Burnaby, Port Moody, and beyond fits the stereotype. In fact, there are some great Lower Mainland watering holes . . . so long as you know where to look. Here's a sudsy roundup of some of the best.

Flying Beaver Bar (4760 Inglis Drive, Richmond; 604-273-0278; www.drinkfreshbeer.com) is part of the group that owns Yaletown Brewing Company, so you can expect a casual ambience encouraging long afternoons of languid quaffing—especially if you snag a table on the patio to catch the floatplanes diving onto the Fraser River. Inside, it's all wood-columned comfort and chatty tables (try for a hearth-side sofa spot) where you can partake of well-selected brews like Sleeman Cream Ale and Red Truck Lager. Food-wise, head straight for the beer-battered fish and chips.

If you find yourself out in Surrey, don't panic. Instead, head for **Central City Brewing** (13450 102nd Avenue, Surrey; 604-582-6620; www.centralcitybrewing.com), near Surrey Central SkyTrain station. Among BC's leading microbrewers—they make award-winning Red Racer Pale Ale—their window-lined resto-bar has a mod bistro feel, complete with glossy wood floors and some cozy semi-circular banquettes. Pints are just $3.50 on Sundays and Tuesdays and nosh highlights include crab spaghetti and bacon-wrapped scallops.

Consider hanging on the fringes of White Rock at **Ocean Park Village Pub** (12822 16th Avenue, Surrey; 604-536-9654; www.oceanparkvillagepub.com), a handsome renovation of what used to be a neighbourhood pizzeria and steakhouse. With its steeply gabled roof and interior of dark timbers, it visually echoes a medieval church. Worship at the booze alter with draft Russell Cream Ale and Okanagan Spring Pale Ale (served in frosted glasses) or, better still, quaff bottles of Tree Brewing's Spy Porter. Comfort pub grub studs the menu, but these guys are still pizza experts: go for the Greek.

The North Shore isn't overly blessed with great watering holes, but among the finest are North Van's **Taylor's Crossing Brewing Company** (1035 Marine Drive, North Vancouver; 604-986-7899; www.drinkfreshbeer.com) and West Van's **Red Lion** (2427 Marine Drive, West Vancouver; 604-926-8838; www.redlionbarandgrill.com). The former is a cavernous but comfy bi-level joint with sports-favouring TVs. Quaff on tasty microbrews like Indian Arm IPA and Mad Scow Stout, then tuck into some beer-braised lamb bolognaise. It's more intimate at the Red Lion, where trad bar décor, including stained-glass panels and carved wood detailing, create a snug, Brit-pub feel. Recommended indulgences here include draft Kronenbourg and a hearty shrimp sandwich.

Also recommended:

Black Bear Pub (1177 Lynn Valley Road, North Vancouver; 604-990-8880; www.blackbearpub.com)

St. James's Well Pub (248 Newport Drive, Port Moody; 604-461-0800; www.stjameswell.com)

Mountain Shadow Pub (7174 Barnet Road, Burnaby; 604-291-9322; www.shadowpub.com)

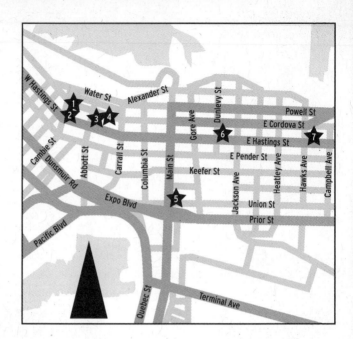

Downtown Eastside

- ⭐ Cambie
- ⭐ Pub 340
- ⭐ Metropole
- ⭐ Bourbon
- ⭐ Brickhouse
- ⭐ Pat's Pub
- ⭐ Au Petit Chavignol

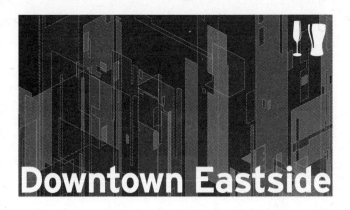

Downtown Eastside

While swanky lounges and sparkling resto-bars continue opening across the city, the Downtown Eastside—here centered on East Hastings but also including Strathcona—is virtually the only place in Vancouver where the kind of grunge pubs that used to line every neighbourhood still exist. In fact, some of them have been reclaimed in recent years as live band haunts or hangouts for young hipsters who don't mind a bit of rough. Of course, not every dive bar is suddenly hip: for every brick-lined, gritty-cool indie joint, there's a stale-smelling, paint-peeled bedlam populated by the permanently wasted.

But the best of the Eastside's old-school bars are the perfect antidote to Vancouver's plastic cocktail spots. Just keep in mind that with Olympics and Woodward's-triggered gentrification, these taverns that time forgot may not be around much longer. For example, the legendary Cobalt was under serious threat at time of research, which is why it's not included here.

When you head down, make sure you adopt the usual Eastside smarts: keep your wallet hidden, avoid the back alleys and stay out of the worst-looking pubs. You'll likely be pleasantly surprised by the 'hood's slightly edgy character bars, its often younger crowd and the low-cost, kick-ass music scene . . . not to mention the cheapest beer in town. And if you need a respite, head further east on Hastings to Vancouver's very best cheese and wine bar, sparkling like a gem in the rough.

Cambie

Grungy old party pub with bargain beer and nosh

Essential tipple Cambie Pale Ale
Must-have nosh Beer & BurgerSpecial
Coordinates 300 Cambie Street, 604-684-6466, www.thecambie.com/v2/bars

Like a grinning, functional alcoholic buddy curling his sticky arms and beery breath around you at a party, the grungy Cambie is regarded fondly by many locals—even if they haven't been here for years. Fans of cheap booze, backpackers from the upstairs hostel and visiting Surreyites eschewing the cover charge at the Blarney Stone keep the place lively, lured by a roadhouse-style atmosphere and a boisterous patio that's the area's best alfresco hangout. Despite its hard-drinking provenance, the sociable Cambie manages to be both edgy and welcoming—a rare combination in any city.

Push through the saloon-style swing doors and step inside for a perch at one of the long communal tables, studded with bent pennies and lacquered with spilt beer. Detritus from the successive bars that have occupied the cavernous space litter the walls, including nicotine-stained paintwork, dusty old TV sets and trailing cobwebs of spent wire. But while there are pool tables and pinball machines—plus a Thursday-night, no-cover DJ—to keep you otherwise occupied, quickly joining the drinkers is the way to go here.

The bargain-priced drafts (only one of which was over $4.50 on my visit) include many of the usual standards (Labatt is cheapest) plus a pair of house-brand tipples made by Granville Island Brewing—the Cambie Pale Ale is best. If you're preciously concerned about grubby glasses, you might like to go for a bottle of Stella, Tiger or Red Stripe instead—just make sure you don your monocle and smoking jacket to sip it in a corner. And if you're wondering how best to stretch your beer budget, Monday offers the cheapest drafts ($3.50 a pop on my visit).

Budget-huggers are also well served by the food menu, which offers a full array of pub grub classics. Almost everything, from perogies to chicken strips and salmon burgers, is under $10 and there are daily-changing specials for a couple of bucks less. The best deal, though, is the permanent nosh special: a $6.50 beer and burger bargain that's likely the cheapest meal deal in town.

Pub 340

Hosting sleepy AA recidivists by day;
a noisy, cheap booze live joint by night

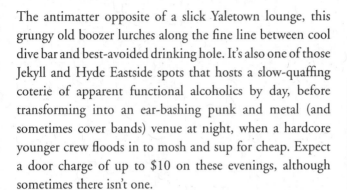

The antimatter opposite of a slick Yaletown lounge, this grungy old boozer lurches along the fine line between cool dive bar and best-avoided drinking hole. It's also one of those Jekyll and Hyde Eastside spots that hosts a slow-quaffing coterie of apparent functional alcoholics by day, before transforming into an ear-bashing punk and metal (and sometimes cover bands) venue at night, when a hardcore younger crew floods in to mosh and sup for cheap. Expect a door charge of up to $10 on these evenings, although sometimes there isn't one.

Locals may remember it as the former Churchill Arms pub. The neon sign is still outside and much of the decor—including a Bavarian-style wooden minstrel gallery—remains in place, alongside a collection of completely mismatched tables and chairs that may have been stolen from other bars when they weren't looking. The stage, which sees band action from Thursday to Saturday, dominates the room. Sit as far back as possible, or in the alcove near the entrance, if you'd prefer to have a conversation with your beer.

The brews, which are predictably cheap, include Russell Brewing's Rocky Mountain Pilsner, Prince George's Pacific Pilsner and a pair of beers from Big Rock, including its bargain-priced, Bud-like Alberta Genuine Draft. Whatever the special is, you can expect to pay around $4.50 for a full, dimple-glassed pint. Alternatively, just get wrecked on Jägerbombs, always priced to move.

Food is served Monday to Friday (although not when the bands are on) and it's of the typical pub grub variety, with a couple of down-market flourishes like hot dogs and all-day breakfasts. Poutine, fish and chips and the hearty mushroom Swiss burgers are ever-popular, but also check the specials board and look out for two regularly occurring favourites: meatloaf and steak with spaghetti.

Essential tipple Pacific Pilsner
Must-have nosh Meatloaf
Coordinates 340 Cambie Street, 604-602-0644

Metropole

Refurbed former dive bar aimed at
the budget-savvy student crowd

Essential tipple Dead Frog Pale Ale

Must-have nosh Turkey Sandwich

Coordinates 320 Abbott Street, 604-408-5822 www.themetpub.ca

The recent makeover of the old Met dive bar could have gone one of two ways. A Yaletown-like gentrification could have transformed the gritty boozer into a slick cocktail lounge. Instead, it's become an exemplar of how to fix up a Gastown bar without abandoning its rough-around-the-edges character. Swankifying the joint might have made better financial sense, but there's method to the madness of keeping it close to the way it was: the Woodward's SFU campus is across the street and the new Met is positioned as its student-luring local.

Step inside the dark, century-old, brick-lined tavern—complete with fire station-style doorways and a crumbling mosaic floor—and you'll find a laid-back younger crowd hogging the heavy wooden tables and black-vinyl bar stools. You might even spot some red-nosed lags from the bad old days who probably haven't noticed the change of ownership.

The newer, study-avoiding regulars spend their time at the bar's arcade machines, foosball stand and pool table. There's even a rare 20-metre-long, sand-covered shuffleboard (it's much harder than it looks). While Friday and Saturday DJ nights are the busiest—there's a $5 cover charge after 10 PM—Wednesday's karaoke shenanigans are also surprisingly popular. You might even hear a snarling, tipsy rendition of *Anarchy in the UK . . .* but only if I'm there (and I've had enough to drink).

The cheap food and beer prices here are a major draw. Alongside the recommended Dead Frog Pale Ale draft are single-can offerings like Colt 45 and Old Milwaukee, the kind of cheap-ass beers beloved of the Met's former regulars. Daily-changing deals include $8 can-and-shot specials plus a heaping $5 spaghetti bolognaise that may be the city's best-value pub grub. In fact, it's hard to spend over $10 on food here: the bulging turkey sandwich and lip-smacking cheddar poutine, made with Guinness-infused cheddar, are highlights. Just because you're a poor student, doesn't mean you have to starve.

Bourbon

Large, old-school tavern with cover-charging
live bands and weekend lineups

A scary, no-go spot less than a decade ago, the brick-cave
Bourbon has cleverly upped its game in recent years,
becoming a popular night-out DJ and live band haunt with
a gritty club feel. Studded with daytime deadbeat drinkers—
plus an honour guard of cashless boozers standing outside
trying to inhale the beer fumes—by night it lures a younger
crowd of in-town suburbanites and students craving a bit of
rough. Bands of the kick-ass indie and/or screaming rock
variety hit the side stage here during most of the week,
when cover charges range up to $10—check the website
calendar and expect to line up on weekends when the party
continues to 3 AM.

The traditional, tavern-like interior of dinged tables and
hardwood floors stretching far back into the shadows like
a tunnel is typical of pubs in this area. But while edging
to the back of less salubrious joints like the nearby Funky
Winkerbeans is not recommended, the latter-day Bourbon
doesn't have any no-go areas. The best seats are the string
of raised vinyl booths on the right side as you enter, while
the twin pool tables will give you something to do if there's
no band on. Check out the giant ducts snaking across the
ceiling: these tubes are used to fire drunks back onto the
streets on really busy nights (just kidding).

Aside from the area-reflecting budget prices, there's
nothing too exciting about the beer selection here. All the
usual domestic bases are hit, including Canadian, Keith's,
Okanagan Spring and the always-cheap Kokanee (it could
never be cheap enough in my books). The bottle selection
doesn't stray much further and as for food: make sure you
eat before you come, since the "menu" here is limited to
five or six different varieties of Lays potato chips. Of course,
beer is all the sustenance you need anyway . . .

Essential tipple Okanagan Spring Pale Ale
Must-have nosh Potato Chips
Coordinates 50 West Cordova Street, 604-684-4214, www.thebourbon.ca

Brickhouse ★

Dive-bar chic meets cozy roadhouse den

Essential tipple Storm Scottish Ale

Must-have nosh More ale . . . or a couple of goldfish

Coordinates 730 Main Street, 604-689-8645

An ultra laid-back clubhouse for students, backpackers and general artsy types, the legendary Brickhouse is not only an oasis from the troubled Downtown Eastside but also from the rest of Vancouver nightlife. Exactly the kind of den-like home-away-from-home bar sorely lacking across the rest of the city, you'll feel instantly chilled out when you push though the inauspicious dive entrance into this windowless cave of brick arches, dog-eared movie posters, twisted fairy lights and the kind of mismatched sagging couches and dinged coffee tables usually found only at garage sales.

If you've turned up on your own soon after the 8 PM opening (they usually run to 1 AM or 2 AM), you'll soon be chatting to the fiercely loyal regulars, perusing the wall-mounted bric-a-brac, peering into the illuminated goldfish tanks and ordering from the sometimes-surly barman-owner, Leo. Almost as legendary as the establishment itself, he's worked hard to keep the place going at the same time as preserving its unique bohemian living room feel. If its takes him a while to crack a smile, just remember that anyone who plays that much reggae and eclectic indie can't be all bad.

Adding to the snug tavern feel—this place has the glowing ambience of a walk-in lava lamp—is a bargain-priced draft list of well-chosen beers from R&B, Shaftebury and Kelowna's Tree Brewing, plus the dark and highly recommended Storm Scottish Ale. And since this is the top end of Vancouver dive bars, you'll also find well-priced highballs and a surprising array of quality whiskies.

Packed with party-hard young out-of-towners on weekends, drop by on Tuesday or Wednesday for the bar's full chill-out effect. Just make sure to eat before you leave home: the late-night bistro upstairs was closed during my visits (possibly for refurbishment) and since the Brickhouse doesn't serve nosh—this is a proper pub, not a restaurant masquerading as a bar—you may start eyeing those goldfish with a slightly esurient look.

Pat's Pub

Great value Eastside bar with surprisingly
good beer and nosh menus

If you're wondering how life could have been if you'd take a wrong turn, check out Pat's Pub during the day. Adjoining the budget-but-safe Patricia Hotel, push though the inauspicious double doors, stroll the gloomy corridor ahead and you'll suddenly hit a quiet, trad barroom with the low-key feel of a working-man's club. In the afternoons, it's studded with lone, sad-faced old lags staring into space at little tables and casting their eyes at the flickering Keno screen. But two unexpected factors make Pat's one of the Eastside's best watering holes: it serves the area's finest beer selection and, by night, it transforms into a youngster-luring live music joint.

And since we're talking about surprises, it's worth noting that Pat's is also one of that small band of Vancouver brewpub brothers. Don't get too excited: it's the ugly brother that never quite succeeded. They only make one beer here—Pat's Classic Lager—and while it's cheap and cheerful, it's not likely to win any brewmaster prizes. But it's an indicator that they take their drink seriously, offering a better selection (at Eastside prices) than any other bar on Hastings. Draft Big Rock Trad, Raven Cream Ale plus Tree Brewing's Cutthroat Pale Ale and Spy Porter were available on my visit.

Up-and-coming thrasher, rockabilly and ska bands—with names like Napalm Willy and Raygun Cowboys—hit the little corner stage on Friday and Saturday nights or you can strut your own stuff here at Tuesday's karaoke session, when the cheap beer fuels a few renditions you'll try to forget the next day. Alternatively, hit the grub. Pat's is the only Eastside bar serving that yuppie staple yam fries, and the rest of the well-priced nosh is similarly above the area's usual fare. Hearty lasagna and shepherd's pie are faves, while the Reuben, beef dip and pulled pork sandwiches also hit the spot. Before you decide, check out the specials board, which can include deals like fish and chips or chicken strips for just $3.95.

Essential tipple Spy Porter
Must-have nosh Pulled Pork Sandwich
Coordinates 403 East Hastings Street, 604-255-4301, www.patspub.ca

Au Petit Chavignol ✪

Perfect cheese-forward wine bar for
a night of indulgent taste tripping

Essential tipple Alvear Amontillado
Must-have nosh Flight of Three "Unusual Ones"
Coordinates 843 East Hastings Street, 604-255-4218, www.aupetitchavignol.com

Eyebrows were raised when this charming little Strathcona spot opened on the wrong side of the tracks in 2009, but Vancouver gourmands have since embraced their regular taste trips to the "other" side of town. Of course it helps that this snob-free but sophisticated eatery-drinkery, which could have graced any city neighbourhood, turns out to be Vancouver's very best cheese and wine bar.

An oasis among paint-peeled storefronts, this lounge-like snug is dominated by its L-shaped, polished concrete bar. Illuminated by pink cuboid lamps, it's ideal for communal quaffing—couples might prefer a candlelit table instead. And if you arrive before the 5 PM opening, nip to next door's large cheese shop for a saliva-triggering taste of what's to come. Both owned by a mother and daughter team known across the city as "the cheese ladies," you'll soon know your palate is in good hands.

With their German family background, the ladies favour riesling and its ability to pair with piquant curdy treats. Dominated by European (especially French) bottles—most available by the glass—there are some additional BC offerings plus a smattering of rich ports, cognacs and sherries (Alvear Amontillado is recommended). And if you're convinced of beer's ability to pair with anything, there are bottles from Leffe, Phillips and Unibroue, plus draft R&B Bohemian Lager. The friendly staffers are also more than happy to offer pairing suggestions.

While many Vancouver bars serve flavour-of-the-moment cheese and charcuterie plates, none come close to the savour-worthy depth on offer here. Up to 20 cheeses are usually available, as well as 10 cold-cut meat treats. It's the cheese, divided into cow-, goat-, sheep- and mixed-milk varieties, that will pique your taste buds. Unless you're a connoisseur, ask for a flight of three "unusual ones" (with wine to match), then sit back and enjoy. If you need suggestions: the ash-covered chevrot cendre and soft maroilles are both excellent, while the amazing robiola a tre latti is the kind of rich indulgence I would happily eat until I explode.

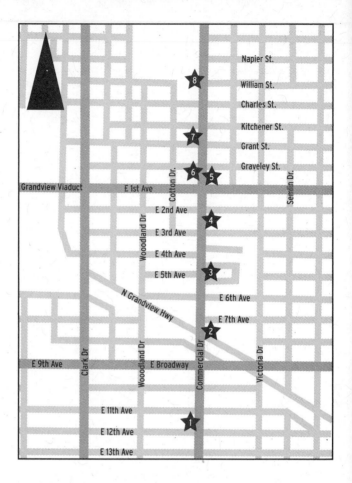

Commercial Drive

⭐ Toby's
⭐2 St. Augustine's
⭐ Timbre
⭐4 Falconetti's
⭐5 Waazubee
⭐6 Avanti's
⭐7 Charlatan
⭐8 Stella's

Commercial Drive

Renowned for its independent, Italian-owned coffee shops, the Drive is also studded with distinctive establishments serving slightly stronger beverages. Bar-curious newbies should allocate the evening for a leisurely booze hop here, perhaps saving time for a sobering java break along the way. And don't worry about trying to recruit a reluctant friend as your designated driver: there's a SkyTrain station stop a short stroll from the main bar action, so you can drink heartily and still find your way back home (leave a trail of bottlecaps from the station to be sure).

While turning south from the Commercial-Broadway SkyTrain station delivers you to Toby's—possibly Vancouver's best-renovated trad pub—most of the Drive's bar action is northwards, between Broadway and Venables, where you'll likely scent a few naughty cigarettes and spot the occasional crazy-eyed hippie scratching his feral beard. A five-minute stroll delivers you to St. Augustine's, with its giant array of regional microbrews, followed by laid-back neighbourhood haunts like Timbre and Charlatan. Further north uncovers sausage-loving Falconetti's; bohemian-chic Waazubee; and Avanti's, an old-school blue-collar pub that feels like a transplant from the suburbs. Best of all is the magnificent Stella's, with its head-throbbing array of Belgian brews.

Toby's

Cavernous neighbourhood pub combining artsy
flourishes with a huge sports screen

Essential tipple Big Rock Warthog Cream Ale **Must-have nosh** Chicken Sandwich **Coordinates** 2733 Commercial Drive, 604-879-2099, www.tobys.ca

Instead of heading to the Drive's usual bar drag when
stepping from the SkyTrain station, turn south along
Commercial and within a couple of blocks you'll be at
Toby's, a giant, immaculately maintained trad boozer with
some surprising aesthetic flourishes. You'll find mosaic
floors, Deco-style stained glass and a series of eye-catching
paintings lining the wood-framed walls—especially upstairs
where there's a huge stylized Vancouver cityscape jostling for
attention with what looks like a garden of Eden populated
by supermodels: if you drink enough, they'll start winking
at you.

But don't be fooled by the art. This is a laid-back,
no-nonsense bar where thirties-and-up locals drink away
their workday woes, especially on hockey and UFC nights
when the city's possibly largest sports screen flickers to life
downstairs. If you're not up for a viewing, decamp to the
hearth-heated patio out front or, better still, clomp upstairs
to the best seats in the house: a row of comfy brown leather
booths. You'll still be able to hear the cover band playing
below on Saturdays and Sundays. Alternatively, bring your
own ukulele for Thursday's open-mike night.

There are 14 mostly well-priced drafts to keep you
hanging around here, including highlights like Strongbow,
Dead Frog Nut Brown and the rare-for-Vancouver Big Rock
Warthog Cream Ale. And although this is primarily a beer
joint, there are a few martinis and signature cocktails if you
need to mix things up—grab an icy Bellini to cool down.

Food-wise, there's nothing too outlandish here and you
can probably guess half the menu before even looking at it.
Burgers dominate—there are nine on offer—but there are
also alternatives like a seafood quesadilla plus several pasta
and stir-fry dishes. If all you want is a good pub grub fill-up,
go for the tasty chicken sandwich. Prepared with bacon and
pesto mayo, it's a Toby's fave that never fails to satisfy the
overly esurient.

St. Augustine's

Cavernous sports bar with a fantastic
array of draft microbrews

Proving you should never judge a book by its cover, this giant but standard-looking sports bar surprisingly offers one of the city's very best selections of draft microbrewed beer, rivalling both the Alibi Room and Backstage Lounge. But the Drive's newest drinkery doesn't pander to the hood's artsy, counterculture vibe. Instead, it's studded with large flatscreen TVs and a plethora of café-style black tables and chairs. There's also a roster of cover-free Friday and Saturday live bands that can range from ska to folk.

Around 20 frequently changing taps jostle behind the bar—check the latest menu to see what's available—and while most are from BC brewers like Storm, Tree, Phillips, Lighthouse and Central City, there are usually two or three celebrated US beers rarely available in Vancouver. On my visits these included tipples from Oregon's Deschutes, Seattle's Pyramid and California's Lost Coast. All are reasonably priced, especially when they're on special for under $5. Even better is the taste tripping sampler of four 4oz glasses for $8.

While the selection is ever-changing here, there are two proprietary brews that usually stick around: St. Augustine's Pilsner (made by Russell Brewing) and the recommended St. Augustine's Stout (made by Vancouver Island's Lighthouse Brewing). And although the owners are not as zealous about chasing down obscure BC brews as the Alibi Room (which is why you'll see Granville Island Brewing beer here but not there), they're serious enough to run their own Monday cask-ale nights.

Food-wise, the selection is not as inventive as the beer menu, although that may change as the bar finds its feet. Dominated by hearty burgers and sandwiches (go for the chipotle chicken quesadilla or crispy chicken parmesan sandwich), there's also that ubiquitous pub standard fish and chips. The starter plates are a little more interesting, so consider a clutch of yam fries, phyllo shrimp and crispy dry ribs to accompany your leisurely beer-supping odyssey. And just in case you were wondering: St. Augustine is the official patron saint of beer and brewing.

Essential tipple St. Augustine's Stout
Must-have nosh Chipotle Chicken Quesadilla
Coordinates 2360 Commercial Drive, 604-569-1911, www.staugustinesvancouver.com

Timbre
Warmer than a log cabin lined with bootleg whisky

Essential tipple Amnesiac Double IPA
Must-have nosh Gut Strut Jambalaya
Coordinates 2068 Commercial Drive, 604-215-7515, www.timbrerestaurant.com

Strolling north on Commercial from the grubby Broadway intersection, you'll be more than ready to slake your thirst by the time you reach the corner of McSpadden Avenue. On steamy summer evenings, Timbre's open-to-the-world roll-up windows make the two sides of this compact, blockish bar appear like one big chatty patio. In fact, the slender, shelf-like exterior perch is usually studded with grinning bohemians knocking them back and tapping their hennaed toes to a CD soundtrack of vintage indie and contemporary bluegrass.

Time your visit accordingly—especially for Jazz Thursdays—and there might even be live performers to wet your whistle: you can stare them out face-to-face inside with a table closely abutting the tiny stage. Cozy in winter, Timbre's interior has a rustic chic élan with wood-plank tables, piquant local artworks and a hefty, log-hewn countertop. It's a warm setting for a few beers, but avoid the ho-hum drafts in favour of an impressive selection of bottled BC treats like Blue Buck Ale, Phoenix Gold Lager and larger shareables such as the lip-smacking Driftwood Ale and citrusy Amnesiac Double IPA (at least I think that's what it was it was called).

There's also an excellent array of shooters and cocktails with naughty names like Cougar, Nipple Flick and Sex on the Drive. Or how about indulging in a little M.I.L.F. action, concocted from Baileys and macadamia nut liqueur? The rabidly hungry are also well catered to here with a hearty gastropub approach that elevates Timbre's nosh well above standard pub fare. Steak and goat cheese salad is a standout while the Gut Strut Jambalaya is packed with prawn, scallop and smoked-chicken goodness. If you're noshing on a budget, Wednesday night's beer and burger special ($12 to $14) also hits the spot rather than the wallet.

Falconetti's

Dark and hopping Drive bar with
a celebrated sausage menu

This legendary little beer and sausage bar (you don't see many of those, do you?) was undergoing a slow expansion into the space next door on my visit and it's hard to say exactly how much things will change when Falconetti's 2.0 is revealed. With any luck, they won't transform into a slick restaurant and they'll keep all the best features that have made this one of Vancouver's unique watering holes. Of course, if they've gone the whole hog and changed into a Milestones clone, you can read this as a nostalgic reminder of what used to be.

In this darkly cave-like hole in the wall, snag a seat at the counter and order from one of the attractive goth-chick girls displaying her tattoos at you like a walking Rorschach inkblot test (yes, we know what you're thinking). As you plug into the room's party-like vibe of animated conversation and indie-cool music (it's like a permanent *Pulp Fiction* soundtrack in here), select from a well-priced pair of Storm Brewing drafts—Hurricane IPA is recommended—or choose a Russell Brewing or Granville Island tipple.

Bottles, including Belgium's Palm Speciale and Kulmbacher Export from Bavaria, add to the selection and there are some minor wine offerings to keep things interesting. Not surprisingly, there's also a good array of tequila, tempting highballs and some standard cocktails. All are ideal as the night winds to a hazy close and the outside lamplight casts a slow glow through the front window . . . although you probably won't notice that if you've disappeared down the tequila route.

Falconetti's eclectic food menu is even more celebrated. Start with some garlic and lime–tossed fries and then dive into one of the eight house-made sausages, served with peppers, onions and house sauce in a soft bun. There's one vegetarian option, but the rest are juicy, mostly spicy meat offerings like Cajun Chaurice, Chicken Thai and Yucatan Chicken. If you're a Falconetti virgin, go for the bulging Hot Italian, a family recipe that's nicely spiced but not too hot.

Essential tipple Storm Hurricane IPA
Must-have nosh Hot Italian Sausage
Coordinates 1812 Commercial Drive, 604-251-7287

Waazubee

Bohemian hangout with good brews, hidden
wine list and lip-smacking bistro nosh

Essential tipple Scottish Ale

Must-have nosh Maple Chili-Glazed Salmon

Coordinates 1622 Commercial Drive, 604-253-5299, www.waazubee.com

The Drive's favourite bohemian haunt is like stepping into
a long cave designed as a quirky art installation. There's a
bent cutlery chandelier, birdhouse light fixtures and dozens
of odd, abstract paintings that invite debate over what
exactly constitutes art. During the day, this all looks a bit
shabby-chic but at night, when soft lighting and flickering
candles illuminate the interior, it creates a sultry haven for
flirty counterculture girls and chin-stroking lads with ironic
goaties. You don't have to be an artist to feel welcome here,
though: Waazubee's is bohemian-friendly but not exclusive.

If skulking in the shadows at the back is not your thing,
angle for a front window seat so you can ogle passing locals.
Toast them with top brews including Crannóg Pale Ale,
R&B's Bohemian Lager (of course) and the dark and creamy
Scottish Ale, made by the Drive's own Storm Brewing. Less-
sudsy lures include a good cocktail array (there's a Bitchin'
Martini that certainly is), plus refreshing, summer-hugging
pitchers of Pimms, served with lemonade, cucumber, mint
and fruit floaters. The wine list, focused on New World
tipples, is also impressive: request 2oz taster glasses to try
a few, then ask about the hidden, off-menu bottles in the
cellar.

Waazubee's nosh is of the hearty bistro variety, with
tempting entrees indicating a Pacific Northwest fusion
approach. Bison burgers are a long-standing favourite
among Commercial's non-vegetarian folk, but the lip-
smacking maple chili–glazed salmon is also recommended.
Lighter shareable fare includes finger-licking yam fries and
hot crab dip. And if you run out of intellectual things to
talk about (who cares about Sartre and Camus anyway?),
the DJs rocking the joint from Thursday to Sunday will
keep you and your partner quiet for a reason.

Avanti's

Blue-collar pub antidote to the Drive's
counterculture ways

If you're hankering after one of those aesthetic-free 1980s neighbourhood pubs that still dot the suburbs, this is the place for you. Grubby carpets (try not to look too closely), red-topped tables and ugly green metallic railings supposedly echoing the brass trims of traditional pubs is the main look here, but only if you can tear yourself away from the TVs and Keno screens flickering from every corner. A blue-collar alternative to the boho bars and dreadlocked neighbourhood surrounding it, this is the kind of place where counterculture Drivers wouldn't be seen dead.

Which, of course, suits the regulars perfectly. Before the feral anarchists moved in, Commercial was a working-class hood and this was the kind of bar that thrived. Now, it's virtually the last one standing. Clamorous with noisy hard drinking on weekend nights, the rest of the time it's just a fancy-free haunt for a few beers and some standard pub grub. And like those quiet saloon areas that used to be a feature of UK pubs, you can avoid the rabble by finding a soft spot upstairs in the lounge—a.k.a., the old smokers' room. With a fireplace and sofas, it's also the only area with windows.

Surprisingly, the draft selection is not just about Coors and Kokanee. In fact, you'll find Strongbow, Russell Cream Ale and Okanagan Spring Lager. A good array of bottles— including Hoegaarden, McEwan's and the recommended Newcastle Brown—round out the main offerings. The food is hearty, traditional and often of the satisfying deep-fried variety, with a full-page of fries-accompanied sandwiches along with pizzas and burgers. Check the specials board for the daily hangover cure or just go the recommended pasta route: spaghetti and meatballs with garlic toast is hale and heaping and is good value at less than $8.

Essential tipple Newcastle Brown
Must-have nosh Spaghetti and Meatballs
Coordinates 1601 Commercial Drive, 604-254-5466

Charlatan

Beer-loaded neighbourhood boozer with
hearty meat-treat entrees

Essential tipple Black Velvet
Must-have nosh Brisket Sandwich
Coordinates 1447 Commercial Drive, 604-253-2777, www.thecharlatanrestaurant.com

Ghostly fans of the former Bukowski's can sometimes be spotted hiding in the shadows at the street corner bar that replaced it. They're the ones with the beer-stained shirts reading dog-eared copies of *Ham on Rye*. But much of the Drive has moved on from its rabid, counterculture days (hence the nearby Tim Hortons) and the Charlatan is a popular reflection of that change.

Possibly Commercial's best neighbourhood pub attracts local hipsters and older barflies in almost equal measure. But although sitting in the darkened interior—especially at the windowless, subterranean back bar that's lined with glossy wood walls—is an easy way to forget the time of day, summer quaffers should arrive early enough for a table on the slender patio that's comfortably fringed with gently rustling trees. It'll keep you cool while you shoot sidelong glances at the eclectic action promenading past on the Drive.

Beer-wise, there's a bewildering draft array of 20 domestic and import brews. Most are fairly mainstream— Sleeman, Granville Island, et al.—but sip-worthy highlights include Grolsch, Strongbow, Whistler Black Tusk and a rich, blended Black Velvet of Guinness and cider. A splash of wines and cocktails round out the selection, but beer is the raison d'être here, especially on game nights when live hockey—that other life-giving force—illuminates the TVs above the bar (check for game-night beer specials to so you can celebrate or commiserate on a budget).

Like the booze menu, the Charlatan has some fancy food offerings (mussels and Thai curry, for example) but it's the hearty carnivore dishes, that salve larger appetites. Dining here is recommended when you're at that dizzy-with-hunger stage: if you're picturing your friends as giant hams, you're ready to eat. Loosen your belt and dive into a pulled pork burger, bacon-studded meatloaf or the excellent, velvet-soft brisket sandwich and you'll soon be questioning the sanity of any vegetarians you might know.

Stella's ✪

Aladdin's cave of astonishing Belgian
brews for true beer nuts

It's 11 AM and you've woken up with a gravely voice, bleary eyes and a head that feels like a melon on a toothpick. Casting your foggy mind back to last night, all you can remember are the words "lambic" and "11.5%," plus a spirited attempt to create a new Belgian anthem based solely on beer. Welcome to the aftermath of a slippery-slope night out at Stella's, a Vancouver pilgrimage spot for fans of the world's best ale-making nation.

The bar at the north end of Grandview Park (there's also a newer Stella's on Cambie—see page 111) has a welcoming, wood-lined interior the colour of golden pilsner. While there's a good side patio for summertime quaffing, hunkering down in a cozy inside corner with the mammoth Fresh Sheet of bottled brews is the best way to spend any winter evening. Draft Leffe, Kronenbourg and Stella Artois are available, of course, but the more exotic Belgian bottles are the main attraction.

The choice is bewildering, so ask your server to match your usual tastes to something on the menu or just plunge in for some eye-popping experimentation. You'll soon be sipping rich, spicy concoctions that make jokes of all those generic factory beers you've wasted your life on. Recommendations include the fruity Mort Subite Kriek; the coppery Chimay Rouge, which tastes like a cinnamon IPA; and the dark and smoothly wonderful X.O., a brooding, end-of-the-night beer made with cognac and lots of love.

Two notes of caution: these tipples are often way above regular strength and some cost northwards of $10 each. If you don't plan to max your credit card on booze, save some dosh for a few shareable plates to soak up all that beery excess. Moules et frites is the way to go at Stella's—there are eight brothy varieties to choose from. As well, cones of crisply addictive fries (served Euro-style with mayonnaise) are a perfect ale accompaniment. And if you need a break from the liquid nectar, try Korean-barbecued short ribs or the appetite-assaulting poutine, made with Blanche de Chambly beer.

Essential tipple X.O.
Must-have nosh Moules et Frites
Coordinates 1191 Commercial Drive, 604-254-2437, www.stellasbeer.com

Ambience: best three . . .

Irish pubs
Doolin's Irish Pub, 38
Irish Heather, 9
Wolf & Hound, 136

Live music joints
Backstage Lounge, 123
Railway Club, 55
Yale, 44

Under-the-radar bars
Black Frog, 15
Fringe Café, 132
Narrow Lounge, 98

Lounges
Afterglow, 24
George Ultra Lounge, 26
Habit Lounge, 102

Hotel bars
Opus Bar, 28
Shangri-La Market
   Restaurant Lounge, 48
Sylvia's Lounge, 67

Dive bars
Brickhouse, 80
Cambie, 76
King's Head, 129

Character bars
Diamond, 7
Pourhouse, 14
Six Acres, 11

Late-night haunts
Bin 941, 71
Corduroy, 128
Railway Club, 55

Game night pubs
Atlantic Trap & Gill, 20
Dix BBQ & Brewery, 21
Toby's, 86

Urban patios
Chill Winston, 4
Five Point, 104
Kingston Taphouse, 56

Waterfront patios
Galley Patio & Grill, 137
Mill Marine Bistro, 62
Wicklow Public House, 114

Cozy winter bars
Cardero's (Live Bait
  Marine Pub), 63
Nevermind, 135
Sylvia's Lounge, 67

**Bars with a great
nighttime vibe**
Cascade Room, 103
Kino Cafe, 110
Subeez, 22

Trad pub ambience
Dix BBQ & Brewery, 21
Toby's, 86
Wolf & Hound, 136

Bars with DJs
Bourbon, 79
Morrissey Irish House, 43
Subeez, 22

Bar washrooms
Chill Winston, 4
O Lounge, 49
Opus Bar, 28

Art-lined bars
Toby's, 86
Waazubee, 90
Whip, 99

Bars with quiz nights
Cascade Room, 103
Library Square, 58
Three Lions Café, 101

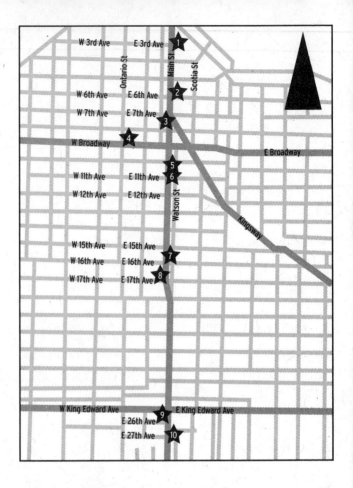

Main Street

⭐1 Narrow Lounge
⭐2 Whip
⭐3 Foundation
⭐4 Three Lions Café
⭐5 Habit Lounge
⭐6 Cascade Room
⭐7 Five Point
⭐8 Public Lounge
⭐9 Locus Café
⭐10 Main

Main Street

Once-gritty Main (here encompassing both the Mount Pleasant and Riley Park neighbourhoods) has been transformed in recent years by a young community of Puma-wearing, ironically goateed new locals that demanded their own indie bars as soon as they began moving in. These area hipsters—they're the ones complaining about the price of Biltmore Cabaret tickets while tapping away on their top-end Apple laptops—have triggered a full menu of some of Vancouver's best original drinking spots. Which is particularly apt, since several historic beer-makers once occupied an area called Brewery Creek near the Broadway and Main intersection here.

Despite the historic provenance, you won't find many traditional pubs on Main. Instead, look out for excellent and often clamorous good-time haunts like the Cascade Room, a great 101 intro to the area's friendly coolsters; the veggie-hugging Foundation, where philosophical conversation starters line the walls; the Brit-owned Three Lions, with its innovative gastropub menu and chatty vibe; and the Whip, an arty neighbourhood bar where the Sunday cask-ale event is a local beer-lovers legend. And then there's the reopened Habit, Vancouver's best '70s-style retro lounge. But wherever you decide to quaff, don't miss the Narrow, a smashing but well-hidden subterranean snug with a cozy, David Lynch look and a free-use turntable.

Narrow Lounge ✪

Dive-bar chic meets Lynchian surrealism at
Vancouver's finest hidden watering hole

Essential tipple Bramble
Must-have nosh Unburger
Coordinates 1898 Main Street, 778-737-5206, www.narrowlounge.com

Eagle eyes are required to find the entrance to this subterranean drinkery, nestled among suspicious-looking, half-closed storefronts on Main. Just scan for the illicit-looking red lamp around the corner on 3rd Avenue, duck through the shady doorway and then descend a short stairwell lined with graffiti artwork. Don't be scared: pushing through the heavy door at the bottom, you'll suddenly emerge into one of Vancouver's most amazing small bars—the kind of eclectic spot that instantly becomes your local, even if you live several kilometres away.

Not much bigger than a railcar, the windowless, mood-lit Narrow is like stepping into a David Lynch dream about a vintage dive bar. Suited dwarves rarely appear, but the room's oddball decor includes bleached antlers, junk-shop pictures, a small neon crucifix and what looks like a mounted stuffed dog's head. Local hipsters love the place, especially for the turntable that plays vinyl from a library that includes Suicide, The Ramones and even the *Cocktail* soundtrack: ask nicely and they'll let you choose an album or two. While the Narrow closes at midnight, it always feels like 3 AM here.

Not resting on its eccentric looks, service is warm and friendly and you'll soon feel at home. Grab a high table facing the bar (there's not exactly much choice) and you'll be staring down a wall of tempting libations. You'll be drawn to the skull-shaped Crystal Head vodka bottle, but cocktails are the drink of choice here. Classics are well represented and expertly prepared—try a great Bourbon Sour or sip on a perfect Bramble (gin, sugar syrup, lemon juice and crème de cassis).

There's also an excellent boutique beer menu with choice mostly bottled tipples, including Blue Buck Ale, Negra Modelo, pop-top Grolsch and stubby Boris from Quebec. The single-malt choice is at least as impressive (go the Oban route). And while you're tucked into your underground bunker don't forget the nosh. Taking a gourmet comfort food approach, highlights include hearty mac and cheese, delicate beet and walnut salad and the top-choice Unburger: a bulging slice of meatloaf on a baguette.

Whip

Friendly, just-off-Main neighbourhood haunt
without the hipster hang-ups

Luring the cool Main Street crowd long before the area's hipster bars rolled in, the Whip is a warm and welcoming combination of old-school pub élan and contemporary, art-lined hangout. The bar's funky paintings are changed monthly, but the chatty patio, intimate mezzanine level and nicely worn, candlelit furnishings are mainstays that make this arguably East Van's comfiest neighbourhood joint. There's an animated chit-chatty vibe here most evenings but the best time to come is Friday night, when a DJ has the place chillin'. And don't miss Sunday afternoons, when a guest cask of BC beer is tapped—it's the best way to spend a long, loungey PM and forget all about work on Monday.

Drinks-wise, the drafts are all from the home province, with a heavy emphasis on R&B and Storm Brewing beers. If you're enjoying the patio in summer—unusually for Main, it's larger than a postage stamp—consider the light and refreshing Phoenix Gold Lager from Phillips. In addition, there's always a rotating local special (you'll have to ask for it) as well as a bargain-priced daily brew—it was Lucky Lager for $3 on my last visit. Intriguing cans and bottles, including the wonderfully dark and malty Paddock Wood Black Cat Lager from Saskatoon, add to the mix. There's also a flirty array of cocktails, including a list themed around the seven deadly sins: lust works for me.

The food is a cut above standard pub grub with an eclectic menu of Whip favourites and fusion temptations. That includes some good vegetarian options like the recommended teriyaki tofu stir-fry. Carnivores will likely prefer the satisfyingly spicy Mexican chicken burger. Alternatively, this is a good spot for some tasting-plate shenanigans—go for the black-bean quesadilla or the addictive sweet yam frites . . . and don't even think about sharing them.

Essential tipple Paddock Wood Black Cat Lager
Must-have nosh Sweet Yam Frites
Coordinates 209 East 6th Avenue, 604-874-4687, www.thewhiprestaurant.com

Foundation
Cozy young intellectuals bar with a vegetarian menu

Essential tipple Scottish Cream Ale
Must-have nosh Utopian Nachos
Coordinates 2301 Main Street, 604-708-0881

Resembling a museum of mismatched melamine tables and vintage vinyl chairs, the city's coolest vegetarian hangout is a great rainy day haunt, especially when the condensation on the windows adds a misty élan to proceedings. Your fellow hunkers will be those bright-eyed twentysomethings that can make 1940s thrift-store clothing look cool and they'll likely be discoursing passionately about their undergrad papers on Foucault. Join in by reading from the pithy philosophy quotes lining the walls—although pretending they're your own musings can lead to problems, especially if you try them on the wait staff (trust me on this).

Despite the intellectual veneer, it's not all serious here and the Foundation is often a buzzing nighttime spot even if you only have half a brain cell. Recently expanded—head around the back and try for the corner banquette table—the chatter here is fuelled by a well-priced bar selection that includes the usual bottled suspects plus some recommended drafts (go for a pitcher to keep things rolling). There's a pair of R&B Brewing tipples as well as four beers from Storm Brewing, including the excellent Scottish Cream Ale. A few New World wines and some basic spirits round out the selection.

Food-wise, this is a rare vegetarian and vegan-only spot. But before you consider sneaking in a bacon sandwich and eating it under the table, check out the menu: there are plenty of home-style dishes here to satisfy most visiting carnivores and their savoury, protein-loving ways. The hearty salad selection includes an excellent peanut-flavoured tofu-satay variety and the "Revolutionary Rations"—otherwise known as mains—include spicy curries and a pair of bulging burgers (try the black bean–packed Bentonio Burger). But the real treat here is a heaping plate of Utopian Nachos piled high with cheese and veggie goodness. It's just what a hungry Marx and Engels would probably order if they happened to stroll in.

Three Lions Café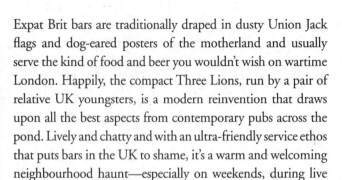

Brit bar with great grub, choice beer . . .
but without the colonial hangover

Expat Brit bars are traditionally draped in dusty Union Jack flags and dog-eared posters of the motherland and usually serve the kind of food and beer you wouldn't wish on wartime London. Happily, the compact Three Lions, run by a pair of relative UK youngsters, is a modern reinvention that draws upon all the best aspects from contemporary pubs across the pond. Lively and chatty and with an ultra-friendly service ethos that puts bars in the UK to shame, it's a warm and welcoming neighbourhood haunt—especially on weekends, during live TV soccer screenings or on Tuesday's busy quiz night.

There's a slender side patio for summertime quaffing here, but the wood-floored, stained-pine interior is the heart of the place. Sit back and take your time choosing your brew: the deceptively tiny corner bar is home to draft Tetley and London Pride as well as bargain-priced Three Lions Lager (it's actually Russell Brewing Lager with a house-brand label). Bottle-wise, you'll find Newcastle Brown and Brooklyn IPA highlights, but there's also arguably the city's best cider selection—including Bulmers, Blackthorn and the celebrated Sir Perry Traditional Pear Cider.

Whatever you do, make sure you come here with a hearty appetite. Three Lions has one of the best food offerings of any bar in the city and you can taste the gourmet gastropub love in slow-cooked, wonderfully satisfying dishes like house-made lamb burgers, bangers and mash served in Yorkshire pudding and a pair of rich Indian-style curry dishes that put many Vancouver restaurants to shame. All meats are organic and as much as possible is sourced locally.

Check the daily specials and make sure you come back in the morning to address your inevitable hangover with definitely the city's best pub breakfast. Served with baked beans and top-notch sausages, eggs and bacon, their Full English feels like your mum made it—if your mum happens to be a professional chef. Of course, if you only need a snack, there's an alternative: bags of imported UK potato chips—including Hula-Hoops—are offered behind the bar just like in the old country.

Essential tipple Tetley Bitter
Must-have nosh Full English Breakfast
Coordinates 1 East Broadway, 604-569-2233

Habit Lounge

Retro funk '70s-look room with fun
cocktails and surprising whiskies

Essential tipple Sex on the Beach **Must-have nosh** Lamb Meatloaf **Coordinates** 2610 Main Street, 604-877-8582, www.habitlounge.ca

Reinvented after the fire that gutted the joint, the new Habit is the city's coolest retro-look lounge. With its '70s cop show soundtrack, you'll be tempted to dive in across the tables like Starsky and Hutch (don't try this; it hurts) but it's better to just chill and enjoy the ironic rec-room aesthetic of chocolate brown walls, fake-wood-grain tables, and a vertical frieze of shag carpeting.

Luckily the vibey L-shaped room isn't just about looks, especially late at night when it takes on a party feel. That's aided by the warm glow from the plastic globe lampshades and the unmistakable sound of cocktails being shaken around the room. While Habit has some excellent bottled beers and a respectable clutch of wines, it offers two unique-for-Vancouver tipple attractions.

There's a 21-choice menu of well-priced Canadian whiskies ranging from Crown Royal and Canadian Club to the lesser-expected Wiser Deluxe, Forty Creek Barrel Select and Potters 15-year Plus. Generally smoother and lighter than their Scottish brethren, they invite revelatory taste tripping. But there's more: order one of five Reinvented Retro Cocktails and the ingredients come to your table in a bento box of measuring jars, an ice-packed serving glass, a recipe card and a little steel shaker. Nothing is more likely to trigger a great atmosphere than giggling drinkers shaking their own cocktail booty. Indulge in a little Sex on the Beach action, chef up a perfect Tequila Sunrise.

Thankfully, you don't have to make your own dinner as well. Habit's compact menu offers clever reinterpretations of retro nosh so well prepared and plated they resemble the front covers of old *Family Circle* magazines. Appie plates of salt cod cakes or sweet carrot and brie perogies are good, but heartier comfort fare is the way to go. Try the pork croquettes or tuna casserole (they're nothing like your mom used to make) or go for the excellent lamb meatloaf, served with pan-fried potatoes, green beans and a tomato Provençal that was the height of dining sophistication when you were a kid and tastes better than ever here.

Cascade Room

Hopping neighbourhood bar with great cocktails and gastropub nosh

Fittingly situated in Main Street's old Brewery Creek area, where the now defunct Vancouver Brewery once cranked out its fortifying beverages, this hopping and highly convivial drinkery combines the best in old and new bar approaches: cool enough to draw the Main Street hipsters, it also offers superb drink and dine menus and manages to feel instantly like your own neighbourhood bar no matter which neighbourhood you actually hail from.

In summer, grab one of the high-chair tables at the open front section to catch the Main Street action or, if it's cold, sink into the vinyl sofa seating and patchwork flock-wallpaper area at the back—especially on Mondays, when the chatty Quiz Night fills the room. Who knew that such a weathered English pub tradition could draw so many? Not surprisingly, there's an even greater vibe here on weekends, when the lively soundtrack (Arctic Monkeys to vintage Cure) keeps things truly buzzing.

With part-Brit ownership—hence the "Keep Calm and Carry On" etching at the front—the beer selection here is top-notch, with choice BC microbrews jostling with international bottled faves like Coopers Sparkling Ale, Young's Double Chocolate Stout and the smashing and nicely hopped Anchor Steam. Even more impressive is the giant, 50-item cocktail menu. All the lip-smacking classics are here—from Mint Juleps to Singapore Slings—but check the board above the bar before you order since there's always an intriguing off-menu special. Save room for the seductive Cascade Room Cocktail. It's bourbon shaken with pressed apple, lime juice, vanilla bean, bitters and egg white.

There's a gastropub approach to the food here that puts the menu on a par with many leading city restaurants. The inventive, seasonally changing selection usually includes roasted halibut, brie-baked polenta and local duck breast but the highlight is the tender, wine-braised beef, served with bubble and squeak (that Brit influence again).

Essential tipple Cascade Room Cocktail
Must-have nosh Wine-braised Beef
Coordinates 2616 Main Street, 604-709-8650, www.thecascade.ca

Five Point

Loungey neighbourhood haunt
with Main's best party patio

Essential tipple Missing Bikini
Must-have nosh Five Point Slider
Coordinates 3124 Main Street, 604-876-5810, www.thefivepoint.com

Nestled incongruously alongside the handsomely turreted Heritage Hall, this sassy spot is like a combination lounge bar and sports pub: step inside and you'll find a pink-chandeliered, black-hued room on your left, while on your right is a trad bar topped with TV screens ever-tuned to the latest game. But the dual approach works perfectly and this is often Main's busiest drinkery—especially in summer, when its hopping patio is the 'hood's best alfresco perch and the thumping club music gives the place a great chill-out vibe.

Of course if it's winter, you'll want to hunker down inside: try for a deep sofa seat around the fireplace or take your group to the elevated bench table at the back so you can look down imperiously on your fellow quaffers. Even better, turn up with your ukulele for Monday's open-mike night and see how quickly you can clear the room with your sparkling, sing-a-long rendition of "Crazy Horses" by the Osmonds.

If you're booed off stage (okay, *when* you're booed off stage) console yourself with a drink or three. There are 14 drafts here, although several are "beer cocktails" like Snake Bite and Black Velvet, while the rest are standards such as Stella, Grolsch, Strongbow and a pair of Big Rocks. A small smattering of wines is additionally available but the tempting cocktails (all reduced by 50 cents a pop on Saturdays) are your best bet. Sink in for a session of Foxy Ladies and Lazy Days or head straight for the Missing Bikini, a highly sippable concoction of Malibu, crème de cacao, coconut milk and fruit juices that triggers sunny vacation dreams no matter how dreary it is in Vancouver.

Nosh-wise, there are the usual pasta and burger entrees alongside a bigger and more tempting array of appies that are ideal for snacking or sharing. Tuna bites, baked brie, Moroccan chicken and spicy wok prawns are popular but go for the tempting Five Point Slider of three mini-burgers instead: blue-cheese beef, ahi tuna in togarashi and grilled chicken in barbecue sauce. It'll fuel you up perfectly for your ukulele encore.

Public Lounge
Intimate, art-studded hangout for tapas fans

Slightly hidden in the no-man's-land stretch between the two cooler Main Street hubs around Broadway and 20th Avenue, this little mod eatery-drinkery is well worth a visit. Inside a bright, woodsy interior of blocky tables and shabby-chic walls studded with local-artist abstracts, slide onto a high-chair perch at the tiny bar and peruse the offerings. Alternatively, consider an alfresco table at the small patio out front—it's fringed with swaying bamboo, but you'll still be subject to the clamorous traffic whistling past just a few feet away.

Before ordering from the menus—which are attached to clipboards to make you feel a like a doctor considering a course of treatment—check the chalkboard specials high up on the wall to the left of the bar. If nothing takes your fancy, delve into a drinks array of fairly standard drafts like Sleeman Honey Brown and Russell Cream Ale, plus Quebec's less-expected Éphémère apple beer. Some international bottles add depth to the selection, including larger sizes of Czechvar and Young's Double Chocolate Stout that, like "beer tapas," are perfect for sharing. Almost two dozen wines—about one-third from BC and most available by the glass—keep non-beer drinkers happy, alongside a decent and well-priced martini list that you'll likely stray to as the 1 AM closing time rolls around.

Recently changing its food offerings from a mains-focused approach to shareable tasting plates, the menu here includes larger tapas treats like turkey meatballs, parmesan-crusted chicken and the recommended sesame-crusted tuna. Also popular are smaller plates of goat-cheese bruschetta, spicy shrimp wontons, beer-broth mussels and tenderloin steak bites. But if you're just looking for some tasty finger food to accompany your leisurely imbibing, check the wall's other chalkboard. You'll find an often-changing list of cheeses, meats and antipastos available for $3 to $4 a pop (minimum order of three). Look out for the ash-ripened chèvre and Hungarian farmer's sausage.

Essential tipple Young's Double Chocolate Stout
Must-have nosh Sesame-crusted tuna
Coordinates 3289 Main Street, 604-873-5584, www.publiclounge.ca

Locus Café
Funky fusion of comfy pub and organic art cave

Essential tipple Chimay Blue Cap
Must-have nosh Miso-glazed Sablefish
Coordinates 4121 Main Street, 604-708-4121, www.locusonmain.com

Like burrowing under the skeletal root system of a mini-forest of mangrove trees, the interior of this instantly cozy candlelit bar is cobwebbed with funky branches sprouting through the walls and ceilings. Peer closer into the shady corners and you'll also spot mask-like faces staring back at you and eyeing your beer. But despite the brooding paintings that also dot the walls, Locus is never pretentious: it just feels like a pub that happens to be art-house cool.

With its large wooden booths, little outside-inside patio and dark boxwood furnishings, this is a highly laid-back spot for a chill-out evening—especially late at night when the eclectic soundtrack (ranging from Piaf to Rasta-jazz on my visit) takes hold and the place becomes a cocoon of comfort. And if you can't find a table among the dense root system, make for a perch at the central wooden bar. You'll soon be chatting to the servers and forgetting the time as the night rolls on to an unexpectedly sudden closing.

By that stage, you may be considering building a treehouse in the branches to spend the night. The late-night drinks specials that kick in after 10 PM have probably led you to this point. Red Truck, Phillips IPA and three ciders—including two from the Okanagan—enliven the draft selection, while the impressive bottles include Duvel, Phoenix Gold, Krusovice Imperial Lager and the dark and malty Chimay Blue Cap. A well-rounded whisky selection and some lip-smacking cocktails (go for the Mumbai) add to the appeal, while the full-page wine list is much better than at most bars.

The varied food menu of international dishes was in transition at time of research—check ahead on the website—but hopefully popular mains like chicken tikka, seafood linguine and the recommended miso-glazed sablefish with spicy kimchi will still be around when you drop by. If not, you could just gnaw on a few roots to keep you going for the night.

Main

Comfy haunt with a Euro-bar feel and great Greek nosh

This instantly cozy, wood-lined bar-café has been a Main Street fixture for years. But while its recent new owners have tweaked the food and drinks array a little, there are no plans to reinvent a wheel that's been rolling along highly successfully. Drop by on a summer afternoon to bask cat-like at the open windows or snag a perch on the tiny side patio outside. In winter, tuck yourself in at a candlelit little table under the latticework ceiling or hit the cocoon-like snug up the steps at the back. This is the kind of comfy neighbourhood hangout you plan to hit for an hour . . . and then end up chatting away the whole night.

Of course the live, cover-free and fairly eclectic music roster helps. Local performers (rarely bigger than three-piece bands) from singer-songwriters to folk and indie acts add a toe-tapping vibe to proceedings from Thursday to Saturday, when you'll notice at least a table or two of family and friends cheering them on. Access a calendar of upcoming live attractions from the bar's website.

While the menus were being revamped on my visit, fave drafts like Stella Artois, Okanagan Spring 1516, Storm IPA and the excellent Strom Black Plague Stout were expected to stick around, mainly to prevent a revolt from regulars. There's also a small but well-chosen bottled array, including the recommended Brooklyn Brewery Lager. A good choice of wines (including some Greek tipples) is available by the glass, alongside a healthy array of classic cocktails like Singapore Slings and mai tais. Check the daily drink specials before you order.

Since the Main's new owners are just as Greek as the former incumbents, you can expect a strong Mediterranean focus on the menu. The ever-popular, velvet-soft roast lamb shoulder hits the spot if you're starving, while a few mainstream non-Greek entrees from the world of pub grub classics are also available. Even better is the menu of well-priced Greek tapas, including finger-licking dolmades, calamari, hummus and pita and a sharp feta cheese plate.

Essential tipple Storm Black Plague Stout
Must-have nosh Roast Lamb Shoulder
Coordinates 4210 Main Street, 604-709-8555, www.themainonmain.com

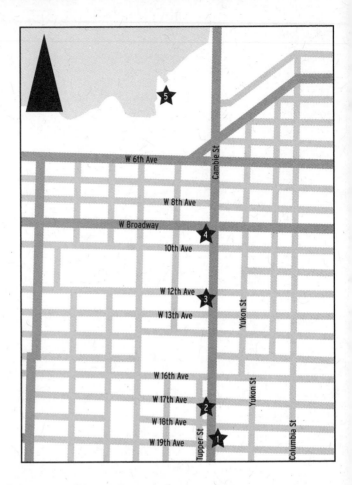

Cambie Corridor

1. Kino Cafe
2. Stella's on Cambie
3. Figmint
4. Original Joe's
5. Wicklow Public House

Cambie Corridor

The opening of the Canada Line presents you with the perfect opportunity for a transit-supported bar crawl. Take the swanky new line to King Edward Station and then stroll north down Cambie Street, with the tree-bristled mountains winking at you ahead. It's up to you how far you want to walk, but if you can't stand the pace you can hop the number 15 bus at any point along the route.

A languid 10-minute saunter brings you to the Kino Cafe, where you can catch hopping flamenco acts before crossing over to the other side of Cambie. Here you'll find the newer of Vancouver's two Stella's, the perfect spot for some Belgian beer quaffing. Hop the bus or keep walking (or weaving) and 10 minutes later you'll be at the loungey Figmint followed by the pub-style Original Joe's.

Jump back on the Canada Line at the Broadway–City Hall Station across the street here or continue downhill underneath the bridge. Inching towards the False Creek waterfront—a stroll best done when it's still light—you'll soon come to the Wicklow Public House. There's a great rooftop patio here, and it's just a short stroll back inland to the Olympic Village Station. Who needs a designated driver when you've got the Canada Line to get you home from a boozy night out?

Kino Cafe

Energetic and highly popular nighttime
haunt for vibe-craving Cambieites

Essential tipple House Sangria **Must-have nosh** Kino Pizza **Coordinates** 3456 Cambie Street, 604-875-1998, www.kinocafe.ca

With the garage windows up and the evening's golden
glow spilling across the wonky tables, dinged boxwood
chairs and paint-peeled walls, it's easy to imagine yourself
in a steamy old-school bar in downtown Buenos Aires
here . . . especially when the little dance floor is clattering
with stomping flamenco dancers and the sangria-fuelled
crowd is in full animated party mode. Welcome to the
Kino, possibly Vancouver's worst-kept barroom secret; an
energetic and hopping little joint that's become so popular
that reserving a nighttime table on Fridays and Saturdays is
essential.

A sleepy neighbourhood bar by day—it opens at 3 PM—
the place transforms every night when a roster of cover-free
live acts hits the stage (keep in mind that when it's especially
busy, a minimum drink and tapas order of $10 is requested).
You can expect toe-tapping little bands of the mariachi
or gypsy swing variety on Mondays; local comedians on
Tuesdays; and full-on dance and music flamenco shows
from Wednesday to Sunday. Get in the mood with a jug
or three of house sangria at your table or knock back a few
glasses of Red Bull Pale Ale, a Kino signature beer made by
Red Rock. Geographically apt bottles of Corona and Dos
Equis also add to the mix.

Feel free to soak up the sunset on the street-side patio
outside. And if watching all that dancing tires you out, tuck
into a large but not overly innovative array of tapas (mostly
priced under $10). You'll find a few bar standards mixing
it up with spicier treats like Spanish meatballs and a simple
but effective plate of bread and chorizo. For heartier fare,
this is also a good spot for pizza, with bocconcini, salmon
and chicken pesto thick-crust varieties luring your taste
buds. Instead, go for the recommended Kino Pizza of ham,
olives, mushrooms and pesto.

Stella's on Cambie

Appealing reinvention of the original, with expanded food and an abiding beer infatuation

Essential tipple Gulden Draak
Must-have nosh Beer-brined Pork Tenderloin
Coordinates 3305 Cambie Street, 604-874-6900, www.stellasbeer.com

Reinventing the kitsch-cool spot formerly occupied by the Tomato Café, the newer of Vancouver's two Stella's perfectly combines art moderne and Canadiana. Step inside and you'll find an alluringly swish old-school bar facing wood-planked walls dominated by an imposing painting of a wilderness stag. Which doesn't mean you have to sit inside: there are two patios here, flanking a museum-like barbershop that couldn't be more incongruous if it was painted pink.

There's an additional dining area inside, but the chatty barroom is the place to hang. Scale one of the high tables or grab a chair at the dineresque counter—the bar seats here are much comfier than at the other Stella's—then cast your seasoned eye over the beer selection. There were 18 drafts available on my visit (with more planned) and they fuse the best of both worlds: Leffe, Kronenbourg, Pilsner Urquell and strong Delirium Tremens highlight the overseas taps, while BC is ably represented by a pair of lovely brews from Phillips (go for the Chocolate Porter).

But like it's older sister, Stella's excels with its amazing bottled Belgians. More than 40 are on offer, plus an ever-changing sheet of specials and rare treats that needs to be carefully perused before making any thirst-slaking decisions. On the main menu, look out for creamy Satan Red, rich Piraat and the celebrated Gulden Draak, a fruity but irresistible 10.5% witches brew often referred to as the world's best beer. Also consider one of the beer and whisky pairing packages (from $13 to $18).

The food menu has been tweaked somewhat from the other Stella's and there's a bigger focus on restaurant-style entrees like crispy duck-leg confit, and a smashing beer-brined local pork tenderloin, served with chocolate porter baked beans and johnnycake cornmeal flatbread. Beer-friendly tapas are still readily available, though, including eight brothy varieties of moules et frites. And if you just fancy something to nibble on with your tipple, check out the cheese and beer pairings—Satan Red with Oka Regular from Quebec is recommended.

Figmint

Comfy hotel lounge bar where you
can have your own private party

Essential tipple Fig Martini
Must-have nosh Crispy Prawns
Coordinates 500 West 12th Avenue, 604-248-4766, www.figmintrestaurant.com

As close as you'll get to a slick lounge around the cheap-as-chips Broadway and Cambie area, the resto-bar of the Plaza 500 Hotel was lavishly swankified a couple of years back. Diners—especially of the hotel guest variety—hit the stripy banquettes in the main room, but quaffers are treated to their own adjoining mod-look drinkery, lined with '60s-style armchairs and a backroom snug accessed through a diaphanous curtain.

Tuck yourself into a smoked-glass table here and rest easy against the suede-lined back wall. And since the atmosphere is entirely dependent on your fellow drinkers, consider bringing a group and concocting your own private party. With an off-the-beaten-path location that's rarely crowded, it can be a good chill-out spot for an evening of chat and flirty libations.

Drinks-wise, the Crannóg drafts that graced the bar in its re-opening honeymoon period have been replaced with three slightly less exciting Okanagan Spring brews. The best of these OK taps is the highly sippable 1516 Lager. Instead, go for a bottled beer: they have stubby Boris from Quebec, rare-for-Vancouver Efes pilsner from Turkey and the excellent Flying Dog Porter from Maryland. A boutique array of wines and an eight-tipple offering of cocktails keeps things interesting—the Fig Martini of fig-infused vodka with lemon and white cranberry juice is highly recommended.

And if you need a refuel on your way down the hill, you can order from the full but pricey restaurant menu (go for the scallops and Berkshire pork entree) or just hit the abbreviated lounge list of tempting tapas. This menu changes a couple of times a year, based on the season, but the crispy prawns with sweet-and-sour squash velouté is a frequently occurring favourite that you won't want to share with anyone—try hiding them in your pockets.

Original Joe's

No-nonsense beer and pub grub watering
hole with a hidden rooftop patio

Hitting all the right bases as a pretense-free, '80s-style resto-pub, this friendly former Fogg 'N' Suds, upstairs at the corner of Cambie and Broadway, is ideal for a few bevies and some hearty grub on your way home from work. Combining saloon-trad brick columns and thick wooden tables with sports bar features like a pool table and hockey-loving TV screens, the best seats in the house are the large corner banquette, the clutch of stools at the bar and the hidden rooftop patio mercifully located away from the exhaust choke of clamorous Broadway.

While Sunday night brings some DJ shenanigans (and the occasional cover band), the thirtysomething crowd is usually just here to fill up on beer and nosh. The three proprietary drafts on offer—go for the Original Joe's Red Ale—are made by Alberta's Big Rock, but additional thirst-slakers include Guinness, Whistler Lager and twin offerings from Aldergrove's Dead Frog Brewery (the Nut Brown is recommended). All are served in proper 20oz pint glasses. Fourteen wines—including several from BC—and some tempting cocktails round out the selection, with the Black Raspberry Sling ideal for winter sipping and the vodka-and-Cointreau-infused Back Porch Lemonade perfect for a summer evening on the patio.

With a large food menu and good-value specials throughout the week, it's hard to go hungry here. The specials include Sunday's $10 pizza deals and Tuesday's $2 tacos, but you can expect a heaping bang for your buck whatever day you roll in. All the usual hearty pub grub suspects are here—burgers, steak sandwiches, chicken fingers, fish and chips, etc.—plus a few surprises like butter chicken, blackened salmon and the recommended bacon-and-prawn-packed jambalaya. Add a steaming bowl of chili corn chowder and you won't have to eat for a week.

Essential tipple Original Joe's Red Ale
Must-have nosh Jambalaya
Coordinates 2525 Cambie Street, 604-434-5636, www.originaljoes.ca

Wicklow Public House

Laid-back clubhouse-style bar with a great patio

Essential tipple Stamps Landing Special

Must-have nosh Crab Cakes

Coordinates 610 Stamps Landing, 604-879-0821, www.thewicklow.com

If you're crawling the Cambie corridor and you've just left Original Joe's, hop on the Canada Line across the street and you'll be back downtown in minutes. Alternatively, continue northwards down Cambie (don't cross the bridge) and make for the South False Creek waterfront. You'll pass Olympic Village station and trip across the old rail tracks before hitting the seawall. Developed in the 1980s, this Stamps Landing stretch is markedly different from North False Creek's glassy towers and it feels like a separate suburban enclave in the heart of the city. Check out the crazy paving and terracotta-brown low-rises, then nip into the Wicklow neighbourhood pub.

Inside the long, narrow interior you'll find an older, lounge-style look combining a black-painted bar, wood-block tables, plank-beamed ceiling and a staff of smiling lady servers. The clubhouse feel appeals to the salty, generally older regulars, many from the boats jostling in the marina or the surrounding clutch of homes. They don't get many non-regulars here off-season and when you step into the "club" there's a definite wife-swapping élan hanging in the air. If you're here in summer, though, head upstairs to the huge rooftop patio with its fantastic views of the boat-studded creek framed by Granville Bridge.

Libations-wise, the standard triumvirate of Irish drafts is on offer and you'll also find taps pouring Stella, Sleeman and the lesser-expected Sapporo. Additionally, there are plenty of bottles, including a larger-than-average array of coolers and ciders. The well-priced wines (go for a full bottle) hit the spot and there are a few tempting cocktails to wet your late-night whistle: the Stamps Landing Special of blueberry vodka, citrus vodka, apple sourz and cranberry juice slides down particularly well.

If your Cambie pub crawl has left you starving by this point, hit the stomach-stuffing Irish stew or braised lamb shank entrees. Lesser appetites should dive into a Cobb salad or partake of an appie or two. The small plate won-ton prawns and three-cheese potato skins are suitably savoury tipple accompaniments, but the thick, crispy rock crab cakes are the way to go.

114

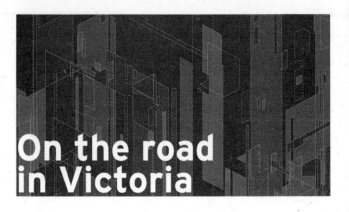

On the road in Victoria

Beer has been on the menu in BC's turreted old waterfront capital since the first thirsty settlers rolled in looking for a drink. But Victoria's sudsy provenance is not lost in the past: today's brick and beam–lined bars make this one of Canada's best pub cities, especially for fans of lip-smacking local microbrews. Here's a frothy round of Victoria's tastiest watering holes.

Spinnakers Gastro Brewpub (308 Catherine Street; 250-386-2739; www.spinnakers.com) is the ideal spot to kick off your leisurely crawl. One of Canada's oldest brewpubs, pull up a window seat, gaze at the floatplanes dive-bombing the harbour and sip on a selection of tasty house-brewed beverages. Highlights include copper-coloured Nut Brown Ale and hoppy Blue Bridge Double IPA.

Spinnakers also mirrors British gastropubs with a soul-food menu focused on regional ingredients. Head straight for the sharable Paysan platters of wild Pacific salmon and Cortes Island clams and you'll momentarily forget you're in a pub at all.

Weaving across Johnson Street Bridge in the direction of downtown, you'll come face-to-face with **Swans** (506 Pandora Avenue; 250-361-3310; www.swanshotel.com), which rivals Spinnakers in the brewhouse stakes. The flower-decked patio restaurant and heritage hotel combo has nestled in its heart Buckerfields Brewery and its chatty, wood-beamed bar. Trains used to run straight into this old grain-storage warehouse, hence the ancient railway track mounted on the ceiling.

Nightly live music keeps the regulars happy, while beer recommendations here include the malty Appleton Brown

Ale—a distinctive brew that'll make you permanently turn your back on Kokanee. Adventurous quaffers should also try the Black and Tan, a heady mix of Oatmeal Stout and Buckerfields Bitter. But save room for a gourmet beer-pairing dessert of Riley Scotch Ale and dark chocolate truffles.

Stroll north from here a few blocks and you'll hit **Canoe Brewpub** (450 Swift Street; 250-361-1940; www.canoebrewpub.com) clinging to the waterfront at the end of Swift Street. Since Victoria often basks in sun even in winter, its curving marina-front patio sees more year-round action than most.

But the cavernous brick interior—an 1894 electricity sub-station building—is also an ideal hunker-down spot when the rain rolls in. Pull up a corner table and wrap yourself in signature brews like Euro-style Red Canoe Lager and mahogany-hued Beaver Brown Ale. Seasonal beers (including a strong Winter Ale) are also a specialty and the diverse menu ranges from wild halibut tacos to stomach-stuffing lamb pot pie.

Also recommended:

Bard & Banker (1022 Government Street; 250-953-9993; www.bardandbanker.com)

Big Bad John's (919 Douglas Street; 250-383-7137; www.strathconahotel.com)

Irish Times (1200 Government Street; 250-383-7775; www.irishtimespub.ca)

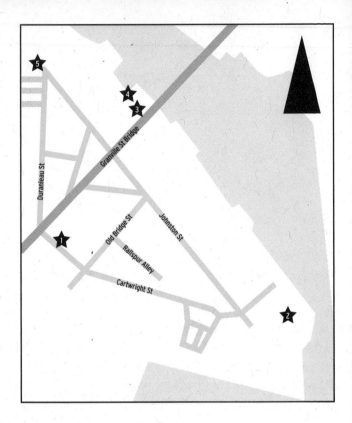

Granville Island

⭐ Granville Island Brewing Taproom
⭐ Dockside Brewing Lounge
⭐ Sandbar
⭐ Backstage Lounge
⭐ Bridges Bar

Granville Island

Tourist-loving Granville Island might have been a great place for illicit hooch in the early 20th century, when it was a grubby nest of gritty workshops and mini-factories known as Industrial Island. But since those hard-drinking days are long gone, contemporary quaffers are forced to sup at a clutch of somewhat more legal joints. And while you won't exactly be planning a 10-stop weave around a giant array of clamorous pubs here, there are just enough interesting bars for a leisurely short crawl. If you need a couple of extras to make a day of it, drop by Railspur Alley: the Agro Café here serves draft Crannóg, while the nearby Artisan Sake Maker offers tastings of its traditional, house-made liquor.

Start your loop at the Granville Island Brewing Taproom (time your visit well and you can take a brewery tour), then weave eastwards along Cartwright Street to the waterfront Dockside Brewing Lounge, one of the city's few authentic brewpubs. Continue westwards from here down Johnston Street and nip into Sandbar for an aperitif. Then hit the nearby Backstage Lounge where a giant array of BC microbrews crowds the bar. You can slide onto the little patio under the Granville Bridge here or continue on to Bridges Bar for a final tipple and a side dish of panoramic sunset vistas.

Granville Island
Brewing Taproom

Bargain beers, a brewery tour and last call at 8 PM

Essential tipple Winter Ale

Must-have nosh Pork Bites

Coordinates 1441 Cartwright Street, 604-687-2739, www.gib.ca

Your first order of business is to take the $9.75 guided tour around the little brewery room, where the legend of Granville Island Brewing began back in the good old days of 1984. While production has mostly shifted to a far larger out-of-town facility, six or seven limited-release bottled beers are still made here annually, often including tongue-tickling favourites like Raspberry Wheat Ale and Ginger Ale (not you grandma's ginger ale, but a zinging alco-version). To stop you from salivating too much, the tour is never too long and you'll soon be perched on the long back table in the Taproom for some generous sampling (tip: they're usually more generous off-season).

But you don't have to take the tour to partake here. The high-ceilinged, timber-framed Taproom has a scattering of wood tables fanning out from a curved bar. Pints are around $4 a pop (a taster selection of four 6oz glasses is also available) and you can choose from the full array of main GIB beers, as well as whatever seasonals and limited releases are available. The adjoining shop is also handy for takeouts.

The mildly hoppy Brockton IPA is the brewery's newest mainstream beer, while old favourites like smooth Cypress Honey Lager and fortifying Kitsilano Maple Cream Ale please most palates. In summer, you'll also want to quaff the refreshing Hefeweizen. If you're here between October and March, though, do not miss the Lions Winter Ale. Arguably GIB's finest, this rich, nicely spiced darker beer is the perfect soul brew solution to one of those long, dark Vancouver stretches.

Since this is a tasting room rather than a full-fledged pub, the Taproom closes at 8 PM nightly and is sometimes shut completely when private functions are on. Also, its food selection is limited to snacks (chips, jerky, pepperoni) and a handful of hot dishes like chicken strips and cheese and bean burritos. But the most popular accompaniment to a hearty round of beers is a plate of breaded pork bites.

Dockside Brewing Lounge

Off-the-beaten-track brewpub with a creek-view
patio and eight unique quaffs

The oft-forgotten sibling of Vancouver's band of brewpub
brothers, Dockside's quiet location at the eastern tip
of Granville Island doesn't help its cause. The attached
boutique hotel and far bigger restaurant room also dominate
proceedings, so the idea that there's a bar up here at all is
often lost. And that's a shame, since this is a good spot to
head on a lazy summer evening, when the golden sunlight is
mirroring off the glassy-calm waters of False Creek and the
brewpub pitchers are flowing on the patio.

Of course, it doesn't have to be summer to visit here.
Dockside's large, wood-accented barroom interior was
recently renovated and now includes lacquered panelling,
a glossy, curved countertop and some sought-after wrap-
around booths that are ideal for hunkering down (if it's
winter, try for the sofas near the log-look fireplace instead).
It's worth getting comfortable so you can sample the eight,
good-value house-brewed beers.

Pitchers are $14 ($9.95 on Wednesdays) but a tasting
flight of six 6oz glasses is the same price and is an excellent
way to taste trip without tripping over. Your choices include
copper-coloured Pelican Bay Brown Ale, dark and moody
Old Bridge Lager and the light and highly quaffable Alder
Bay Honey Lager, made with BC honey. Save room for a
finale glass of fruity Jamaican Lager, suffused with hints of
hibiscus. A thirst-quenching, summer-friendly drink, it's
arguably the brewery's best tipple.

Naturally, there's a full arsenal of classic martinis and
alluring cocktails as well as a nice boutique array of wines
that leans heavily on BC wineries. But sticking to the beer
is a smart move, especially if you take a breather with some
nosh. Those who are starving can hit the main restaurant
menu, but the bar offers its own simplified version to hungry
patrons. Beer-battered fish and chips and Sockeye salmon
burgers are popular but try the chunky chowder or a Sonoran
quesadilla. Made with chorizo, feta and jalapenos, it'll leave
you with just enough room for another round of beer.

Essential tipple Jamaican Lager
Must-have nosh Sonoran Quesadilla
Coordinates 1253 Johnston Street, 604-685-7070, www.docksidebrewing.com

Sandbar

Upstairs waterfront bar favoured
by partying professionals

Essential tipple Sandbar Martini
Must-have nosh Miso-soy Sablefish
Coordinates 1535 Johnston Street, 604-669-9030, www.vancouverdine.com

A swanky, multi-beamed loft restaurant popular among local professionals and Granville Island tourists, Sandbar also offers a casual lounge bar with views of False Creek and the bridge's looming girders. Snag a perch at the horseshoe-shaped counter under the ceiling-mounted fishing boat or sink into a saggy leather chair near the baby grand piano. You'll find someone languidly tinkling the ivories here Sunday to Thursday. But you might want to save yourself for Friday or Saturday nights when DJs spin '80s dance tracks and party-dressed over-30s kick out on the little dance floor. If you're under 25 (male or female) expect to receive lots of flirty attention.

There's a giant, almost bewildering wine menu—aimed primarily at restaurant diners but fully available in the lounge—and you'll have your work cut out studying the dozens of options, many from New World locales like California and Australia. Since most are available only by the bottle, it's easier to choose from the much smaller per-glass selection. Beer-wise, you'll find 12 mostly mainstream drafts (there's even Molson Canadian for the tourists), with Red Truck Lager being your best bet. The weekend dance crowd also likes to knock back a few cocktails: try the recommended Sandbar Martini of vodka and Alize passion-fruit liqueur, shaken with cranberry and lime juice.

If you need a refuel before hitting the dance floor for another vogueing session, you can order from the restaurant's celebrated seafood entree list or pop a few rolls from the on-site sushi bar. More casual bar fare of the salmon burger, scallop kabob and shrimp dumpling variety is also available but the delectable main-menu miso-soy sablefish, served in a lime marinade with rice and veggies is the way to go. And if you manage to snag a sugar daddy (or sugar momma) on the dance floor, maybe they'll even buy it for you.

Backstage Lounge

Great microbrew selection and nightly live
music in a laid-back setting

Essential tipple Bowen Island Cream Ale
Must-have nosh Thai Mussels
Coordinates 1585 Johnston Street, 604-687-1354, www.thebackstagelounge.com

A formerly forgettable spot famed for its cougar action, the Backstage Lounge has quietly transformed itself in recent years. Not only does it have a moody new interior of black leather chairs and cool boho light fixtures, its bar is bristling with 24—count 'em, 24!—draft BC microbrews, a sudsy cornucopia of delights rivaled only by Gastown's Alibi Room. Not everything has changed here, though. There's still that little waterfront patio, always in the brooding shadow of the rivet-studded Granville Bridge, and there are still local live bands on stage every night (cover $5 to $15).

But first, the beer. Staring like a bewildered, drooling senior at the colourful, mostly unfamiliar taps on the counter doesn't make your choice any easier, so just jump in and order the one nearest you. Even many of the regulars—this is Granville Island's neighbourhood local after all—can be as clueless as the visiting ESL students and confused tourists when it comes to selecting a quaff here.

While the selection changes based on availability, you'll usually find choice brews from regional auteurs like Lighthouse, Dead Frog, Red Truck, Tree Brewing, Whistler Brewing, R&B and even the new Turning Point Brewery with its Belgian amber-style tipple. One of the best is the smooth Bowen Island Cream Ale—especially on Tuesdays, when it's often a budget-friendly $3 a glass.

There's also a bigger-than-average shooter, cocktail and wine selection here, plus a pub grub menu that has a few unexpected highlights. Three brothy mussel dishes are offered (the coconut-based Thai variety is recommended), plus popular salmon burgers and pizzas—the Tandoori-chicken variety hits the spot. But if you just need a side-dish fuel-up between brews, go for an order of yam frites or a slider plate of three mini-burgers. If you consume too much, you can work it off on the little dance floor/mosh pit when the band hits the stage.

Bridges Bar

View bar in the heart of Granville Island tourist-ville

Essential tipple Granville Island Ice Tea

Must-have nosh Smoked Salmon Pizza

Coordinates 1696 Duranleau Street, 604-687-4400, www.bridgesrestaurant.com

While the large, yellow-painted restaurant is a long-standing fave with Island tourists (hence the slightly higher prices), there's also a separate, lesser-known bar at Bridges that's great for a couple of brews, a shareable pizza and a spectacular panoramic view of the Burrard Bridge and tree-lined North Shore mountains. Sadly, the higher-paying restaurant crowd hogs the best outdoor seats and the bar's own patio is a small, penned-in area near the building—if you can't see the vista through the throng, consider building a tower of tables to stand on.

All is solved, of course, when the tourists leave town and the packed-up patio area becomes a moot point. Hunker down by the fireplace near the window on a comfy sofa and you can gaze as much as you want at the views. Drinks-wise, Bridges carries most of the Granville Island Brewing family (although it's worth remembering that they charge about $2 more per glass than the Taproom a couple of minutes' walk away). Alternatively, there are a few bottles worth going for, including the tart Okanagan Pear Cider.

But if you've snagged a summertime patio spot, consider a cocktail pitcher to share: the Pimms Cup is ever-popular while the Granville Island Ice Tea (Stoli Razberi vodka, sweet tea and cranberry juice) is a dangerously sippable alternative. Also check the specials list: there's a different cocktail deal almost every night of the week.

The bar's nosh menu includes a few popular dishes from the restaurant, although prices are a little more than most locals would pay for pub grub. Still, the oyster burger and halibut and chips are hearty and satisfying, while the shrimp and salmon burrito is also worthwhile. Better still, is to share a pizza: the shrimp and asparagus variety is good but it's the smoked salmon that hits the spot. And if you're chilled by the winter view outside, go for a Bridges specialty: a steaming, fortifying bowl of seafood chowder.

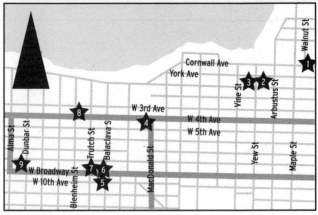

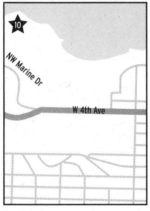

Kitsilano

1. ⭐ Corduroy
2. ⭐ King's Head
3. ⭐ Abigail's Party
4. ⭐ Darby's
5. ⭐ Fringe Café
6. ⭐ Elwood's
7. ⭐ Shack
8. ⭐ Nevermind
9. ⭐ Wolf & Hound
10. ⭐ Galley Patio & Grill

Kitsilano

Often regarded as a nightlife wasteland, the middle-class residential stretch from Burrard to UBC is dotted surprisingly with more than a few bars well worth checking out . . . alongside others that hardly make any effort to lure drinkers living further than 10 feet from their entrances. For the most part, the best bars sadly evade the area's sterling seafront vistas (with one notable exception), instead typically favouring storefront locations on Yew Street, 4th Avenue and West Broadway.

So long as you know where to go, don't let the area's humdrum bar reputation put you off. But also don't expect to wander around and stumble on a great place to drink: this elongated stretch is not amenable to idle crawling, so make sure you have a little geographic method to your drink-crazed madness. Try Broadway for the legendary Fringe Café; 4th for the cave-like Nevermind; the fringes of West Point Grey for the highly amenable Wolf & Hound; and just over the Burrard Bridge for Corduroy, a narrow, kitsch-cool tavern that could grace any neighbourhood. And if you're really keen on a crawl, try the Kits Beach end of Yew with its pair of distinctly different watering holes just a few steps from each other.

Corduroy ✪

Perfect kitsch-cool snug with gourmet
comfort nosh . . . and boot-shaped beer

Essential tipple Corduroy Lager

Must-have nosh Better Than Your Mum's Meatloaf

Coordinates 1943 Cornwall Avenue, 604-733-0162, www.corduroyrestaurant.com

Just the kind of coolly eclectic joint that's been sorely lacking in Kits, this smashing little snug just over the Burrard Bridge could easily be at home on South Main. Lined with junkshop kitsch—apparently chosen to match the golden-wood furnishings—you can expect to gaze upon carved masks, framed mirrors and a series of rubbish landscape paintings that must have been pried from an old lady's basement suite. But it all seems to work, especially when the candlelight casts an intimate glow over the tiny bar with its backdrop of wooden shingles.

Size is an issue here on busy nights, when the long row of bench seating and little high tables can be packed. But the crush fosters a cozy, private-party vibe. And several times a week, they even find room for bands to wedge themselves in between the velour ship painting and the front door. It's less crowded on Mondays when cheap beer mixes perfectly with a bring-your-own-vinyl night.

Like its eclectic decor, Corduroy's menu requires more than a cursory glance. Libations-wise, there's draft Guinness and a pair of Big Rocks, but don't miss the Corduroy Lager. Actually Pacific Western Pilsner from Prince George, it's served in kitschtastic boot-shaped glasses. If you're manhood is challenged by the fey drinking vessels, gruffly order a bottled brew instead—you'll have Red Stripe, Caribou Genuine Draft and a pair of Natureland Organics to choose from. There's also a clutch of enticing, well-chosen cocktails and martinis—go for a Screwed Shirley of vodka, 7-Up and Giffard Cherry Brandy liqueur.

The gourmet comfort food is just as inviting. BC crab and asparagus risotto is excellent, while a side of root-veggie fries is never the wrong thing to order. There's also a late-night menu (they're usually open to 2 AM) that includes a finger-licking roast mushroom, caramelized pear, Gorgonzola, pine nuts and crème fraîche pizza. But nothing tops the velvet-soft Better Than Your Mum's Meatloaf: organic beef with Parmesan, chive potato mash and three-mushroom gravy. It'll have you howling at the moon on your way home.

King's Head

Wood-lined trad pub that hasn't changed in 500 years

A medieval-themed pub that actually looks like it might have been around in the 1500s, the legendary old King's Head has seen better days, but it's still a charmer that's streets ahead of other "Brit-style" bars. Don't expect a Disney version of an old-world pub either: the clapped-out floorboards, scratched-to-crap dark-wood tables and grungy, timber-framed interior is just the kind of look that taverns of yore really had—in fact, they should add straw to the floor and hire toothless crones to make it truly authentic.

In summer, ye olde decke outside is the place to be, but winter quaffers prefer hunkering down at the cozy upstairs booths inside or in the large, main-level quaffing room. In an alternate existence, this might have served as a banquet hall but now it's home to a giant sports-friendly TV screen. Live cover bands also strut their stuff here from Thursday to Saturday. Consider turning up in fully Henry VIII regalia for a spot of stage-diving.

Luring a combination of liver-challenged old regulars and students attracted by the value-priced beer—go for the Sunday to Thursday $4.50 pints of King's Head Lager (made by Pacific Western)—there's a better than average array of brews on offer. Satisfyingly served in full 20oz pints, you'll often find draft Dead Frog Honey Brown, Okanagan Spring Bavarian Lager, Shaftebury Cream Ale and the smashing Granville Island Winter Ale. There's also a good bottled array and a surprisingly large offering of martinis and cocktails (this is Kits, after all).

Food-wise, although this seems like the ideal place to gnaw on giant drumsticks before burping and tossing them over your shoulder, the selection leans more to standard North American pub nosh. With many dishes priced under $10, you'll find steak and kidney pie, salmon teriyaki and cheese steaks, along with possibly the city's biggest burger selection. The 15 varieties on offer include ostrich, caribou, moose and buffalo. Since they're open every day expect Christmas, you'll have plenty of time to try them all.

Essential tipple King's Head Lager
Must-have nosh Caribou Burger
Coordinates 1618 Yew Street, 604-738-6966

Abigail's Party

Intimate lounge room where you new
best friends are at the next table

Essential tipple Abigail's Mojito
Must-have nosh Duck Confit Sliders
Coordinates 1685 Yew Street, 604-739-4677, www.abigailsparty.ca

There's a snug neighbourhood wine bar feel to this tiny Kits eat-and-drinkery that's mercifully linked only by name to the excellent but excruciating Mike Leigh play. Instead of a bullying host and the possible heart attack of your partner, you'll find smiley servers, a glossy-brown candlelit interior and a chilled-out loungey approach in both looks and vibe. It's the perfect place to hang late at night—which is handy, since it's open to 2 AM.

Lined with a handful of little tables facing the bar and kitchen hatch, such an intimate room depends entirely on the night's clientele for its feel. A gaggle of romantic couples can create a quiet, romantic vibe, while a surfeit of chatterboxes can easily trigger a party atmosphere: you'll likely get to know your neighbours very well before the night's out since you'll either be eavesdropping or talking with them soon after you arrive.

If you're looking for a drink (who isn't?) your first order of business is to peruse the blackboard and its ever-changing array of more than a dozen available wine specials. While a few BC treats jostle for attention with international tipples, you'll spot a couple of surprises that are well worth trying: all the blackboard wines are available by glass or bottle. In addition, there's a more permanent cellar list to make your choice even harder. Avoid the stress of choosing with a well-priced Red Truck draft beer or a "party pleaser" cocktail—Abigail's Mojito is recommended.

You'll also be tempted by the gourmet comfort nosh, much of it made with locally sourced ingredients. If you're starving, try the falafel burger, Moroccan chicken or BBQ beef brisket. But if you just fancy some tasty sides to augment your imbibing, go for lamb-sausage corn dogs or the excellent duck confit sliders: toasted French bread piled high with sweet-glazed shredded duck and topped with pickled cabbage strips. Don't order to share or there'll be a massive fight over the third one.

Darby's

Old-school neighbourhood haunt
with great rooftop patio

Tucked along Macdonald just off 4th Avenue, this trad joint feels like a social club for the kind of die-hard, red-nosed locals that have been propping up the bar for decades. Despite being in the heart of Vancouver's yoga-loving, SUV-driving yuppie district, it maintains a comfortable, blue-collar élan, right down to its Keno screens, iron-legged tables and sports-loving TVs screens (we're not taking about flat-screens either: that's a hulking projection TV in the corner).

But while the laid-back interior is an easy place to while away an evening, the best summertime seat is up top. Darby's little rooftop patio, complete with its own small bar, is a great spot for a golden-hued nighttime session. Although, you might want to head back downstairs for Tuesday's comedy or Wednesday's karaoke evenings (or maybe not). Like most Kits bars, you'll find mixed drafts like Crown Floats, Black and Tans and the lesser-known Blonde and Tan (Stella and Guinness) available alongside standard quaffs such as Okanagan Spring's 1516 and the darkly pleasing Rickard's Red.

You'll also find a huge array of cocktails, highballs and martinis not usually seen outside a classy 1970s steakhouse (think King Kongs, Caesars, Pina Coladas, Monte Cristos and a Florida Tracksuit of raspberry sourpuss liqueur, Absolut Mandarin and Shark energy drink). Check for the daily drinks specials or drop by on Sunday when all the week's specials are repeated in one hangover-triggering day.

The food at Darby's has moved on from the greasy pub grub of previous years and now includes intriguing items like Louisiana catfish and chips and "English pub-style curry." The highlights, though, are still the classics. A slight variation on a beef dip, the tender shaved steak sandwich is justifiably popular and slides down nicely with a couple of cold ones—just don't drink too much on karaoke night or you'll be shattering the windows with your "Wind Beneath My Wings" rendition.

Essential tipple Rickard's Red
Must-have nosh Shaved Steak Sandwich
Coordinates 2001 Macdonald Street, 604-731-0617, www.darbyspub.ca

Fringe Café

Honest, ultra-friendly Kits haunt with a cozy
feel and a giant bottled beer selection

Essential tipple Dirty Girl Pale Ale

Must-have nosh Sherpa's Pie

Coordinates 3124 West Broadway, 604-738-6977, www.fringecafe.ca

Although it's only been here since 1990, the tiny Fringe feels like an ancient throwback to Kits' counterculture past. Funkily lined with old licence plates and pop-kitsch posters—yes, that's Reveen opposite the bar—it's also the friendliest watering hole in the 'hood. The staff greet you like you've just walked into their home and you'll soon be chatting with the regulars (they're the ones hogging the spots at the counter) as if you've been coming here for years—a novelty rarely found in many Vancouver drinking spots.

In summer, you can vie for the single patio table out front, but in winter it's all about the cozy, windowless back space or one of the miniscule side tables, each topped with a telephone converted into a lamp. Save time to peruse the Wall of Shame photos near the washrooms and ask the barman exactly what you need to do to get on it yourself— you might have to perform in your Chicken Lady outfit at the monthly open-mike music night.

There's a surprisingly large booze selection here, making it the kind of place where you drop by for one drink and end up staying for 17. The six drafts include Lighthouse stout and IPA from Vancouver Island plus a pair of proprietary beers made by Russell Brewing, which are on $3.99 special every night: take your pick from Ugly Boy Lager and Dirty Girl Pale Ale (go for the Dirty Girl). In addition, there's a good array of single malts and a huge selection of several dozen mostly international bottled beers, including Hobgoblin, Tuborg, Sapporo, Tyskie and Pilsner Urquell.

You'll need to decipher the one-page food menu carefully, since its home-style pub grub selection comes with a Fringe twist. "Damn it Jim!" is actually a grilled cheese sandwich; "Renewable Resource" is a veggie nutburger; and "Che Burrita" is a bean and veggie burrito. Instead, go for the hearty "Sherpa's Pie" (shepherd's pie) for an energy-giving fuel-up before you get back to your Dirty Girl.

Elwood's
Grungy old joint with a laid-back den feel

This grunge-tastic old Kits legend still packs 'em in most nights—although it's quite small so it doesn't take much. The regulars love its comfortably clapped-out interior of scuffed plank floors, chunky wood tables and that familiar aroma of stale beer and caked grime: Elwood's is exactly the way a dive bar should look without actually being a dive. Mixing partying UBC students and thirtysomething blue-collar regulars (yes, there are people with real jobs in Kits), it's a cave-like, windowless old boozer where you'll only see the light of day if you sit on the tiny patio or near the entrance.

Settle in for a night of hard quaffing and you'll have a dozen of so drafts to wet (or maybe drown) your whistle. Keep it cheap with a few $3.99 glasses of Pilsner Old Style—you know you love it, or at least your dad did—or graduate up the quality scale with Grolsch or Big Rock's Rock Creek Cider. Pitchers are well priced and there are some great booze specials every night. There's also a small array of wines and cocktails if you want to mix it up a bit.

Slow down your imbibing with some pub grub. The menu here hits all the usual buttons, with wings being a particular favourite. There are six different sauces available, including Tandoori, Jack Daniels BBQ and the recommended Green Thai Curry (Tuesday is wings special day at 50 cents a pop). Your alternatives include a pulled pork sandwich or a chicken burger rolled in your chosen wing sauce—told you the wings were popular. But the best bet is the appie-sized tuna bites: tasty chunks of blackened tuna steak, served with wasabi sauce. If those don't fill you up, drink more beer or dive into an order of poutine and repeat after me: fat is the new thin, fat is the new thin . . .

Essential tipple Rock Creek Cider
Must-have nosh Tuna Bites
Coordinates 3145 West Broadway, 604-736-4301, www.yourlocals.ca

Shack

Sports-loving party bar popular with
students and local teams

Essential tipple Rickard's Honey
Must-have nosh Tofino Pizza
Coordinates 3189 West Broadway, 604-738-5551

One of the first bars UBC freshers discover when they finally
make it off campus, this Broadway party joint would fit
right in on the Granville Strip (which they usually discover
a few months later). An often raucous, good-time joint on
weekends, when student pleasure drinkers mix and mingle
with local sports teams from the uni and beyond, you can
expect a thumping soundtrack and lots of not-so-subtle
flirting. Decamp to one of the two patio decks to plan your
strategy and you might even pull—try the father figure
approach if you're the wrong side of 30.

The booze list is well priced here, although don't expect
too much in the way of sophistication. Molson Canadian
and a pair of Rickard's brews are the main draft offerings
(go with Rickard's Honey) or you can pick up an ice bucket
of three Corona bottles. Bargain-priced daily specials
abound—$10 jugs were on offer on my last Wednesday
visit. There's also a party-priced array of cocktails, including
some with suggestive names like Golden Speedo, Mr.
Moustache and Single Lady (guys: ask loudly at the bar for
a Single Lady and see what happens).

Burgers and pizzas dominate the standard nosh menu,
with the tasty Tofino Pizza (a new take on the Hawaiian)
winning plenty of fans. It's an ideal accompaniment to a
sports broadcast—the Shack is a popular joint on hockey
and UFC nights. They also have a thing about pulled pork
here: it's added to the mac and cheese dish and it's also piled
onto the nacho plate. And just to show you that students
can eat anything and still look good, there was a taco pizza
daily special on the blackboard on one of my visits.

Nevermind

Darkly cozy underground bar with good
nosh and great hibernation potential

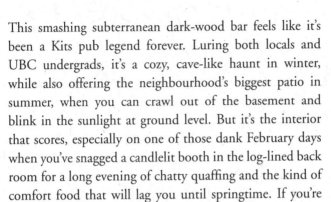

Essential tipple Nevermind Lager
Must-have nosh Spiked Crab and Spinach Dip
Coordinates 3293 West 4th Avenue, 604-736-0212

This smashing subterranean dark-wood bar feels like it's been a Kits pub legend forever. Luring both locals and UBC undergrads, it's a cozy, cave-like haunt in winter, while also offering the neighbourhood's biggest patio in summer, when you can crawl out of the basement and blink in the sunlight at ground level. But it's the interior that scores, especially on one of those dank February days when you've snagged a candlelit booth in the log-lined back room for a long evening of chatty quaffing and the kind of comfort food that will lag you until springtime. If you're embarrassed about eating so much hibernation fuel, draw the little curtain separating each booth here.

Satisfying both of its main demographic groups, the drinks list combines good value tipples as well as a few higher quality treats. The drafts include pairs of Sleeman and Okanagan Spring offerings, plus a pricier pint of exotic Sapporo if you fancy something different. Instead, go for the Nevermind Lager, actually BC's own light and quenching Shaftebury 420. A few wines are also on offer but it's the well-priced cocktails (also available by the pitcher) that are your best bet for a beer-free alternative: go for a Cuba Libre rum and coke highball of Havana Club, coke and a mint garnish.

Food-wise, Nevermind fuses pub fare with some lip-smacking temptations that would easily be at home in a higher-end eatery. The burger selection, for example, combines standards as well as the less-expected and recommended lamb burger. It's a similar story with the pizzas—try the Tuscan. But the best meal starts with a delectable spiked crab and spinach dip starter followed by a mahi mahi taco main. This is also a good spot for visiting veggies: many of the entrees here can be concocted in meat-free versions.

Wolf & Hound

Perfect Irish-style pub with a welcoming
vibe and plenty of good sups

Essential tipple Limerick Lager
Must-have nosh Lamb Roast
Coordinates 3617 West Broadway, 604-738-8909, www.wolfandhound.ca

Close enough to UBC that you might want to consider taking a few classes, this lovely, laid-back bar could teach North America's mostly woeful Irish hostelries a thing or two about Gaelic hospitality. The decor helps: instead of leprechauns and shillelaghs, there's a bright, warm interior of copper-coloured walls, dinged wooden tables and a generous smattering of armchairs inviting you to take a load off. Even the plastic brickwork has a certain charm, especially if you follow it to the giant-screen, sports-loving TV room, which feels exactly like a sofa-lined den in someone's home.

Luring assignment-avoiding students and chore-escaping locals, this is a great place to catch the game with your buddies. Or to bring your dad when you need to ask for extra study allowance money—just make sure you ply him with a drink first. Keep the costs down with the pub's bargain-priced Limerick Lager (actually brewed by Winnipeg's Fort Garry Brewing) or hit the usual Irish suspects of Guinness, Kilkenny, Harp and the less-seen Smithwick's Red Ale. You can try all four in a 5oz sampler that's the same price as a single pint. And it's not just Irish booze here: among the BC drafts is the excellent Storm Black Plague Stout.

There's live Celtic-ish music from Thursday to Saturday (the Cellar Jazz Club is next door if your jigging days are over) while the pub grub food array hits all the right buttons and has a homemade approach. If you're preparing for a long winter on the Isle of Arran or you're just sick of eating mac and cheese every night in res, consider a hearty portion of lamb stew, Guinness and steak pie, bangers and mash or shepherd's pie. Better still: drop by on Friday when there's a great lamb roast dinner special.

Galley Patio & Grill

Chatty, club-style family bar with
jaw-dropping inlet views

A friendly, fancy-free gem hidden from everyone except the Kits locals who've been coming here for years, this laid-back upstairs spot at the Jericho Sailing Centre is one of the only West Side perches where your beer comes with a side order of mountain-fringed waterfront vistas. Arrive early on summer evenings for a plastic table on the large patio and you'll have a mesmerizing, sigh-triggering sunset view across the tanker-studded briny. It's one of the very best panoramas of any bar in the city. In fact, if you've managed to snag a patio spot, consider auctioning it off to the highest bidder when you leave.

The Galley isn't just some boozy old pub for doddering sea salts. One of those rare examples of a true, family-friendly joint (which means you can partake of a side order from the ice-cream counter with your brew), the interior is divided between a bright café-style room that's open to everyone and a fireside Member's Lounge lined with dark-wood tables, softer upholstered chairs and a flotilla of sail-shaped boating trophies. And if you're here on the first Tuesday of the month, try gate-crashing the folk-music jam session in the adjoining room (a thick sweater and a straggly beard should get you through the door).

Beer rules the drinks menu here and there are several taps from the likes of Rickard's and R&B (go for their seasonal Sun God Wheat Ale, if available). Not surprisingly there are no cocktails but since this is Kits, you'll find a few wine offerings—mostly from BC vineyards—aimed at slaking the thirsts of those Lexus SUV drivers that dominate the neighbourhood. And while the food is not particularly cheap, there's a home-cooked feel rather than a nasty fast-food approach to popular dishes like beer-battered fish and chips, mac and cheese (add the chorizo sausage) and slow-roasted barbecued pork sandwiches. Seafood is the recommended route, though, and the oyster po' boy is only slightly surpassed by the pan-seared halibut tacos served with house-made mango-papaya salsa.

Essential tipple Sun God Wheat Ale
Must-have nosh Halibut Tacos
Coordinates 1300 Discovery Street, 604-222-1331, www.thegalley.ca

On the road in the Okanagan

Bleary-eyed and hungover after some ill-advised late-night carousing in Vancouver, I hopped a short mid-morning flight to Kelowna for a hair-of-the-dog Okanagan Valley break. Dripping with more than 100 wineries—including the celebrated likes of Mission Hill, Blasted Church and Nk'Mip Cellars—I planned to drop in on a couple of my usual grape-based faves . . . as well as a pair of lip-smacking beer spots.

With a local buddy serving (somewhat grumpily) as designated driver, I was soon pushing through the wooden doorway of **Summerhill Pyramid Winery** (4870 Chute Lake Road, Kelowna; 250-764-8000; www.summerhill.bc.ca). After a swift stroll around the property—including a visit to the large concrete pyramid where owner Stephen Cipes ages his organic wines—I snagged an alfresco patio table to drink in the views across the rolling, vine-striped hills.

A fruity afternoon glass of Gewurztraminer hit the spot perfectly, followed by a little Peace Chardonnay Icewine. Not usually a fan of the sweet dessert tipple, it's possibly the best I've ever sipped, complete with surprisingly subtle sugars and a deep apricot finish. As a die-hard apricot addict, I was easily won over.

When I returned to town, I arrived at **Freddy's Brewpub** (948 McCurdy Road, Kelowna; 250-491-2695; www.mccurdybowl.com), a chatty locals' haunt. Led by brewmeister Jack Clark, the short brewery tour here illuminated the detailed beer-making craft and included five tasty, shot-sized samples. The light Back Country Lager and slightly hoppy Lord Nelson Pale Ale were good but the dark, brass-coloured Brownstone Ale was easily my favourite.

After a late lunch the next day, I dropped in for a liquid dessert at **Tree Brewing** (1083 Richter Street, Kelowna; 250-717-1091; www.treebeer.com), one of BC's favourite microbreweries. Following a 45-minute guided tour of the bustling operation, thirsty visitors can wind down in the little tasting bar. While the tour includes four tastings and a souvenir glass, visitors can also roll in at the bar anytime for a free sample.

Kelowna Pilsner and Thirsty Beaver are Tree's most appealing brews for microbrew virgins. But I preferred Cutthroat, a sharp, copper-coloured English-style draft, and Hop Head, a flowery, full-bodied India pale ale. I also enjoyed an extra sample of Hefeweizen, an unfiltered seasonal wheat beer ideal for summer quaffing.

Overlooking the vine rows tumbling towards the lake, I finally rolled into **Quails' Gate Estate Winery** (3303 Boucherie Road; 250-769-4451; www.quailsgate.com). A three-tipple tasting here is free—the rhubarby Chenin Blanc and pleasantly peppery Reserve Pinot Noir are recommended—while its BC-focused restaurant is a good spot to soak up any overindulgence. I chose a butter-soft sablefish before finishing with a glass of vintage foch . . . plus some blue, Camembert and smoked cheddar cheeses. Not surprisingly, my belt went into full strain mode.

Also recommended:

Blasted Church (378 Parsons Road, Okanagan Falls; 250-497-1125; www.blastedchurch.com)

Mission Hill Family Estate (1730 Mission Hill Road, West Kelowna; 250-768-7611; www.missionhillwinery.com)

Nk'Mip Cellars (1400 Rancher Creek Road, Osoyoos; 250-495-2985; www.nkmipcellars.com)

Nightcap:
an appendix of BC brewers

Don't restrict yourself to a 100-mile liquid diet when you're craving a BC brew—Pacific Western Brewing in Prince George, for example, is 488 miles away. But do support our regional beer makers whenever you spot their taps or bottles in city bars. Excluding brewpubs, here's a list of large and small province-based producers. If you find any others, please visit www.drinkingvancouver.com and let me know.

Bowen Island Brewing www.bowenislandbeer.com
Cannery Brewing www.cannerybrewing.com
Central City Brewing www.centralcitybrewing.com
Crannóg Ales www.crannogales.com
Dead Frog Brewery www.deadfrogbrewery.com
Driftwood Brewing www.driftwoodbeer.com
Fat Cat Brewery www.fatcatbrewery.com
Fernie Brewing www.ferniebrewing.com
Granville Island Brewing www.gib.ca
Gulf Islands Brewery www.gulfislandsbrewery.com
Hell's Gate Brewing www.hellsgatebrewing.com
Howe Sound Brewing www.howesound.com
Kamloops Brewing www.kbbeer.com
Lighthouse Brewing www.lighthousebrewing.com
Mt. Begbie Brewing www.mt-begbie.com
Nelson Brewing www.nelsonbrewing.com
Okanagan Spring Brewery www.okspring.com
Old Yale Brewing www.oldyalebrewing.com
Pacific Western Brewing www.pwbrewing.com
Phillips Brewing www.phillipsbeer.com
R&B Brewing www.r-and-b.com
Red Truck Beer www.redtruckbeer.com
Russell Brewing www.russellbeer.com

Shaftebury Brewing www.shaftebury.com
Storm Brewing www.stormbrewing.org
Tin Whistle Brewing (no website at time of publication)
Tree Brewing www.treebeer.com
Turning Point Brewery www.turningpointbrewery.com
Vancouver Island Brewing www.vanislandbrewery.com
Whistler Brewing www.whistlerbeer.com

Bar index

Cheers

I'd like to thank all those who not-so-reluctantly joined me at various points on my enforced Vancouver bar crawl, including Dominic Schaefer, Glenn Drexhage, Peter Mitham and Noel MacDonald. I'd also like to thank my brother Michael in the UK for giving up some of his valuable vacation time and coming over whenever possible to join me for a few rounds—I know it's always tough to tear yourself away from your regular JD Wetherspoon pubs. Kudos are also due to Ruth Linka at TouchWood Editions for taking on this project and noticing that I probably wouldn't be too drunk to see it through. Additional cheers go out to Christopher Poon, Andrew Poon, Erin Aldridge, Emily Armstrong, Wendy Underwood and Nigel Springthorpe for their excellent suggestions of bars they thought I should try. And, finally, please note that while this project fuelled an orgy of merry and extended imbibing, no livers were intentionally harmed during the writing of this book.

About the author

Born in the leafy southeast England city of St. Albans (home of what is reputedly Britain's oldest pub), John first nipped across the pond for Expo 86, where he particularly remembers the Elephant & Castle bar with its red telephone box. Returning to study at the University of Victoria a few years later, he eventually swore allegiance to the Queen—in English and French—and became a Canadian citizen. Since 1999, John has been a full-time travel and feature writer and his work has appeared in more than 150 different publications around the world, including *National Geographic Traveler*, *CNN Traveller*, the *Los Angeles Times*, the *Globe and Mail* and the *Guardian Weekly*. He has also written 15 Lonely Planet guidebooks and is the author of *Walking Vancouver*, covering 36 short strolls around the city and beyond—the perfect hangover cure accompaniment to this book. To read his latest stories and peruse current projects, visit www.johnleewriter.com.